8 MIRACULOUS
MONTHS
IN THE
MALAYAN JUNGLE

8 MIRACULOUS MONTHS
IN THE
MALAYAN JUNGLE

A WWII PILOT'S TRUE STORY
OF
FAITH, COURAGE, AND SURVIVAL

DONALD J. "DJ" HUMPHREY II

DJH INC

1221 Bower Parkway #208

Columbia, SC 29212

www.DJHINCPUB.com

DONALD J. "D J" HUMPHREY II

8 MIRACULOUS MONTHS

IN THE MALAYAN JUNGLE

A WWII Pilot's True Story of Faith, Courage, and Survival

Cover Design: Rebecacovers

Library of Congress Control Number: 2020920704

ISBN

978-1-7358451-0-4 (Paperback)

978-1-7358451-1-1 (Hardcover)

978-0-578-77101-4 (eBook)

978-1-7358451-3-5 (Audiobook)

BIO034000   BIOGRAPHY & AUTOBIOGRAPHY / Aviation & Nautical

BIO008000   BIOGRAPHY & AUTOBIOGRAPHY / Military

BIO038000   BIOGRAPHY & AUTOBIOGRAPHY / Survival

Printed in the United States of America

First Printing 2020

First Edition 2020

10 9 8 7 6 5 4 3 2 1

I dedicate this book to Lt. Col. Donald J. Humphrey, my father, a World War II United States Army Air Force pilot. I also dedicate this book to all members of the U.S. Military—both active and veterans—who risk their lives to preserve our freedom.

LT. COL. DONALD J. HUMPHREY
U.S. ARMY AIR FORCE
MEDALS OF HONOR

The Silver Star
Distinguished Flying Cross
Purple Heart
Air Medal
World War II Victory Medal
Asiatic-Pacific Campaign Medal
American Campaign Medal
American Defense Service Medal

Back Row – Left to Right
Major Donald J. Humphrey – pilot
Capt. Earl J. Nelson – co-pilot
(Lt. Col. Robinson Billings sat in for Nelson)
Capt. Carl A. Hansman – navigator
1st Lt. William F. Duffy – bombardier
1st Lt. Ernest C. Saltzman – flight engineer
1st Lt. Martin J. Govednik – radar

Front Row – Left to Right
T/Sgt. Michael A. Kundrat – radio operator
T/Sgt. Harold A. Gillett – left gunner
S/Sgt. John A. MacDonald – top gunner
T/Sgt. Ralph C. Lindley – right gunner
S/Sgt. Rouhier E. Spratt – tail gunner

CONTENTS

INTRODUCTION

It is some story – so fantastic you probably won't believe it. But it really happened.

Lt. Col. Donald J. Humphrey

My father's quotation above is from a press release by the Associated Press and printed in the Iowa *Postville Herald* on September 12, 1945. World War II had just ended, and my father was in Singapore. The press wanted to know what happened to him in the Malayan jungle for the past eight months.

This book tells that story. My father wrote the original manuscript when he was in his 20s. I remember seeing it when I was a young kid— 8 x 10 pages with a thick black paper cover. He always wanted someone to write it better and make it into a published book, but he never found the right person to do it. Then time ran out on him. I decided to dust it off and turn it into a book that would take the reader into the realities of World War II and at the same time tell my father's story of faith, courage, and bravery.

I wrote this book for my father who hopefully is looking down with an approving smile. I also wrote it for my father's family and friends. But actually, I wrote this book for everybody—a fascinating first-person account of a B-29 bomber pilot and an inside look at an extremely important part of history.

1

CHAPTER 1

The Mission

During World War II, I was a 26-year-old Major in the Twentieth Air Force (20th Bomber Command), 468th Bombardment Group of the United States Army Air Force. I was a B-17 and B-29 flight instructor, a veteran of 17 prior bombing missions, and Commander of the 793rd B-29 Superfortress Squadron flying out of the U.S. Army Air Force base at Kharagpur, India. And I was the pilot of B-29 No. 42-24704, the *Postville Express*.

On January 11, 1945, there were 47 B-29s operating out of the Kharagpur base in Northeast India. We took off on our missions in four-plane formations to bomb the Japanese-occupied dry docks at the Naval bases around Singapore Island 1,900 miles away.

These missions were the longest B-29 Superfortress flights ever flown, a 3,800-mile round trip. Each plane could only carry four 1,000-pound bombs to save fuel consumption and make the extended mission possible.

At the halfway mark of the flight, the squadron was on course and schedule when things took a turn for the worse. The weather reporters back at the home base in India had forecast the weather wrong along the flight path. Halfway down the east coast of Malaya, the B-29s encountered unexpected icing conditions and dangerous updrafts and downdrafts that decimated many of the B-29s. Because of the unforeseen weather, only 25 of the 47 B-29s in the squadron made bombing runs on their designated targets in Singapore.

The B-29 No. 42-24691 with Captain Johnson at the controls flew into some extreme turbulence. The four 1,000-pound bombs broke loose from the bomb rack shackles during a violent uplift and fell into the South China Sea. Having lost his bombs, Captain Johnson aborted the mission and returned to base.

Captain Bores, the pilot of B-29 No. 24487, fought a downdraft that took his bomber and crew from 25,000 feet to 15,000 feet. Minutes later, in an updraft, they shot back up to 18,000 feet, and then the turbulent winds pushed the B-29 back up to 25,000 feet. This strong turbulence caused severe damage to the flight instrument panel, making the plane even more challenging to control in the adverse weather. The violent change in direction ripped the radar operator's seat from the floor and threw him against the wall, and the plane's life raft popped open inside the plane. During another violent updraft, the four 1,000-pound bombs snapped out of the bomb rack shackles, broke through the bomb bay doors, and fell into the open waters below. Left with no weapons and a crippled ship, Captain Bores, like many other captains, aborted the mission and turned back for the home base in India 1,000 miles away.

The severe turbulence pushed the *Postville Express* from 25,000 feet up to 32,000 feet in just seconds, and the cold, wet weather coated the wings with ice. However, we could still fly and leveled off to 25,000 feet again. We continued unscathed toward our target 800 miles away.

Because of weather damage, three of the four B-29s in my formation needed to abort the mission and return to the base at Kharagpur, India. Determined to complete the mission, I continued, even though we were now alone without all the machine gun firepower of a full four-plane formation to defend against the Japanese fighters we would encounter. We were the only plane to reach our designated target, King George VI Graving Dock.

We were flying at 23,000 feet over the Strait of Johor, a water body between the southern tip of the Malay Peninsula and Singapore Island. The shining sun was in stark contrast to the severe weather encountered earlier on our flight along the Peninsula's east coast. Across the glimmering Strait in the early morning hours of January 11, 1945, I could see Singapore Island coming into view.

As I turned the *Postville Express* toward Singapore, our target lay just ahead. We flew over the Admiralty IX Floating Dock at the expansive Sembawang British Naval Base of Singapore. This British base fell into Japanese possession when they occupied Malaya in 1942. The Japanese now used it as a repair shop and refueling station for the Japanese Navy's fleet of battleships, heavy cruisers, and destroyers.

The dock looked minuscule from 23,000 feet above, and the Japanese heavy cruiser *Takao* in dry dock there looked like a child's toy. Nearby, damaged in battle and dry-docked for repairs, lay the heavy cruiser *Myoko*, one of their lead ships. Its top deck was erupting in flames from its anti-aircraft batteries aimed straight at the *Postville Express*. Neither of these warships below, however, was our target. Our mission was to bomb the King George VI Graving Dock that serviced the most significant ships afloat and was vital to the Japanese naval war effort. We were finishing the job after sections of the dock survived an earlier bombing raid on November 5, 1944.

As we neared the target area, I banked the *Postville Express* and steadied her for the bombing run. We flew through heavy anti-aircraft flak bursting all around us, but the *Postville Express* flew on, miraculously unscathed.

The plane interphone communication system came alive to

complete the bombing mission.

"Navigator to pilot: The heading is two-one-zero."

"Pilot to navigator: Roger."

Just as the flak subsided, all hell broke loose.

"Top gunner to crew: Six bogies at three o'clock low."

All our heavy machine guns were firing at Jap fighters coming from every direction. Several thousand feet below, I could see 25 more Jap fighters headed upward toward us.

While the gunners were busy with the fighters, 1st Lieutenant William F. Duffy and I concentrated on the bombing run. Duffy was the bombardier who sat below me in the bombardier seat in the front window bubble.

"Pilot to bombardier: Has the ice on the bomb bay window melted yet? Can you see the target through the bombsight?"

Duffy focused all his attention on the window, hoping the ice would either melt or blow off as we approached the target. It was not happening.

"Bombardier to pilot: Negative. Can't see a thing."

"Pilot to bombardier: When you can see the target through the bombsight, advise. Otherwise, it will be a radar drop."

As Duffy pulled back the bomb bay lever, he said, "Roger. Bomb bay doors open."

"Pilot to radar: Prepare for radar drop."

1st Lieutenant Martin J. Govednik, the radar operator, concentrated on his radar scope. It revealed the outline of Singapore Island and King George VI Graving Dry Dock in the northeast corner.

"Radar to pilot: Roger. Three degrees right."

"Pilot to radar: Roger."

I was now flying the B-29 under the radar operator's guidance as we zeroed in on the target.

"Radar to pilot: One degree right. One minute to drop."

"Pilot to radar: Roger."

Duffy placed his hand on the bomb release lever as he waited for word from Govednik.

"Radar to bombardier: Five seconds to drop."

Duffy timed the five seconds and then released the bomb load.

"Bombardier to pilot: Bombs away."

I held the ship on course for another 60 seconds to give the automatic camera time to record the four 1,000-pound bomb hits.

As the bombs left the bomb bay, three Zeros came at us head-on, rolling over onto their backs and firing their machine guns. Just before ramming us, they split and dove underneath us.

Tech Sergeant Ralph C. Lindley, the right gunner, drew a bead on the lead fighter. Squeezing off a quick burst, he observed a puff of smoke emerge from the plane and shouted, "I got one!"

Staff Sergeant Rouhier E. Spratt, the rear gunner, shouted, "Good shooting! It's a flamer. It's going down into the Strait."

Top gunner Staff Sergeant John A. MacDonald yelled, "Here comes another one at ten o'clock high!"

Left gunner Tech Sergeant Harold A. Gillett said, "Yeah, I see him!"

As the Jap fighter drifted back toward eight o'clock, not more than 50 yards from our plane, Gillett riddled it with .50 caliber bullets.

Now Zeros and Oscars filled the sky. The Jap fighters raced to be in position ahead of us and above us. Then they turned back around and dove straight toward our plane with machine guns blazing. When the fighters almost reached us, they released aerial phosphorus bombs in front of us with long chains dangling and spiraling outward to entangle our spinning propellers. My stomach tightened as the speeding fighters swarmed around us with these flaming weapons. All I could think about were the thousands of gallons of gasoline in the wing tanks.

Enemy fighters streaked past the cockpit windows on both sides. My co-pilot, Lieutenant Colonel Robinson Billings, and I ducked. Both of us waited for the explosion, but none came. The fighter plane pilots misjudged the 700 miles per hour combined speed of the airplanes and missed us.

The tail gunner, Staff Sergeant Spratt, watched the flaming

phosphorus spewing in all directions as the aerial bombs that just missed us were exploding behind the plane. With his bird's-eye view from the tail gunner's seat, Spratt, through the phosphorus bomb bursts, watched our bombs detonating around the dry dock below.

"Tail gunner to pilot: We hit the target. Bull's-eye!" Spratt reported with enthusiasm.

"Pilot to tail gunner: Thank you for that excellent report, Spratt."

The celebratory distraction was only momentary as Staff Sergeant MacDonald, the top gunner, shouted, "Six o'clock and coming fast!"

Spratt fired at the swooping Oscar as it flew by. The fighter was so close Spratt said he could see the staring face of the Japanese pilot.

The alerts came hot and heavy over the interphone.

Duffy yelled, "Bandits, twelve o'clock!"

"Two o'clock high! Watch out!" shouted MacDonald.

Lindley cried out in an irritated, intense voice, "Missed him. He's coming round again! I'll get the bastard!"

With all the gunfire and phosphorus bombs exploding around us, the *Postville Express* did not appear damaged anywhere where it hurt. All systems still worked fine, and the gunners were registering an incredible number of hits with their pair of .50 caliber Browning M2 machine guns on each turret. Spratt blew several Oscars out of the sky, and MacDonald, Gillett, and Lindley also scored some hits. The fighters, still not deterred, kept coming.

I turned to Billings in the co-pilot's seat and said, "They said Jap fighter strength would be weak in this area. Where in hell are these guys coming from?"

"You're right," Billings replied. "They gave us the wrong dope at the briefing. We knew there would be some, but not this many."

Duffy, sitting in the front window dome of the plane, was the only one to observe an odd-looking, different-colored grey fighter coming straight at us out of the sun. Duffy was firing his two .50 caliber machine guns at a standard silver Zero at eleven o'clock when the tinted grey Zero at one o'clock high caught his attention. Duffy spun around and trained his guns on the grey fighter, now 900 yards away and closing fast. As soon as the Zero was in the crosshairs of his sights, Duffy fired. The grey Zero never swerved. It came right at us with guns blazing and did significant damage to the *Postville Express* as it soared by a scant 50 feet above us.

Then, WHAM!

The warning klaxon started blasting, signaling the pressurized cabin had ripped open. Dust flew throughout the plane as piercing cold air came rushing in.

I grabbed my oxygen mask and held it over my face. I yelled over the interphone, "Oxygen masks on! Everyone! Oxygen masks on now!"

I did not know what happened, but whatever it was, I knew it was severe. Hearing a low moan, I turned to my right and saw that a Jap fighter had shot my co-pilot, Billings. He was conscious and able to hold his mask on, but I could see blood oozing out of his flight suit around his left knee. He would need a tourniquet to stop the bleeding, and fast.

I pulled my oxygen mask down and shouted across to him, "Are you alright?"

Billings was in a daze but nodded and shouted back, "Okay, but I hope I don't lose this leg. It's a damn good one!"

I glanced to my right at the plexiglass dome and saw a bullet hole right over Billings' head. I could feel my feet sending me a strange message. There was no pressure on the rudder pedals. They were loose, which meant damaged and useless rudder cables.

I yelled over to my co-pilot, "Billings! Try your controls!"

Billings reached out with his undamaged leg to check if his rudder pedals worked.

"No good! They're out!" he yelled back and put his oxygen mask back on.

He slumped back in his co-pilot seat and appeared to be going into shock.

"Pilot to engineer: Billings has a wounded leg. Take care of him the best you can. He needs a tourniquet."

I turned on autopilot, which we nicknamed George, to put the plane into a steep dive and gain more airspeed so we could outrace the fighters. After reaching 15,000 feet, I adjusted the autopilot control to bring the aircraft back to level. As we were leveling off, 1st Lieutenant Ernest C. "Cliff" Saltzman, the flight engineer, came on the interphone.

"Engineer to pilot: Look at number two engine. I think we are losing it."

I twisted in my seat to inspect the engine. It was vibrating but otherwise appeared to be undamaged.

"Pilot to engineer: Feather number two, and calculate how far we can fly on three engines."

"Engineer to pilot: Roger."

"Bombardier to pilot: My guns are out. They will not fire."

"Right gunner to pilot: Mine won't fire either."

"Top gunner to crew: The guns are out. Repeat, the guns are out."

I realized they damaged the Central Fire Control System, which meant all the machine gun turrets were useless except for the tail gunner turret that operated on a separate system. The lone gray Nip did his job.

"Top gunner to pilot: Guns will track, but don't fire."

Tech Sergeant Gillett broke in, "What are we supposed to do? Spit at them?"

"Pilot to gunners: Track them anyway. Maybe it will deter some of them."

Three Zeros from twelve o'clock high came at us in a towline attack with guns blazing. All three fighters hit their target, riddling the plane with hundreds of bullets.

Sitting there in the plexiglass nose, I felt helpless staring at the Zeros coming right at me with machine guns blaring. I felt like I was sitting in a goldfish bowl. It looked like everything was going to hell, and fast.

Saltzman, the flight engineer, was busy working on Billings' leg to stop the bleeding. Tech Sergeant Michael A. Kundrat, the radio operator, tossed Saltzman a first aid kit. Saltzman tied a tourniquet around Billings' upper leg, applied some sulfa powder to the wound, and packed it.

Jumping back into his seat, Saltzman calculated how far the plane could fly on three engines. After doing a few computations, he called, "Engineer to pilot: We can get to within 300 miles of Calcutta and ditch in the Indian Ocean."

"Pilot to engineer: Roger."

Noticing the sky in front of the plane seemed empty, I asked the crew to look around.

"Pilot to crew: What about the fighters? Do you see any?"

Several of the crew replied, "Negative."

Just as I relaxed a bit, I heard, "Right gunner to pilot: Number three engine is on fire."

"Pilot to engineer: Look at number three. Tell me how bad the fire is."

Saltzman looked out his window and responded, "Engineer to pilot: It looks bad. I think we should shut it down."

I replied, "Shut number three down and feather."

"Engineer to pilot: Roger."

"Pilot to engineer: Close the cowl flaps, and use fire extinguisher number one."

"Engineer to pilot: Roger."

Because I knew flying on only two engines would increase fuel consumption, I added. "Also, calculate how far we can go on two engines."

"Engineer to pilot: Roger. Fire's out on number three."

"Pilot to engineer: Roger."

Then I spotted two B-29s flying about a mile ahead of us, one with a feathered number two engine and the other with the bomb bay doors hanging open. I prayed we could catch up with them because we needed their machine guns for defense if there were any more fighter attacks. But with only two engines, I knew there was no way the *Postville Express* could do it.

Saltzman came on the interphone. "Engineer to pilot: I figure we can go about 500 miles, but it looks like we will have to ditch in the ocean."

"Pilot to engineer: Roger."

Hearing this, Captain Carl A. Hansman, the navigator, plotted a course and said, "Navigator to pilot: Five hundred miles will put us in a safe zone. Use heading zero one five."

"Pilot to navigator: Roger."

Glancing out his window, Saltzman was horrified to see flames streaming from the number three engine and shouted, "Engineer to pilot: Number three's on fire again."

"Pilot to engineer: Use the other fire extinguisher."

"Engineer to pilot: Roger." Saltzman pulled the lever controlling the number two fire extinguisher system and said, "That's the last fire extinguisher."

Using the last fire extinguisher appeared to have snuffed out the fire. But only seconds later, Saltzman shouted, "Engineer to pilot: Number three is on fire again!"

There were 2,800 gallons of gasoline in the flaming right wing. It would be a miracle if it did not blow. I now knew we would not make it back to our home base 2,000 miles away at Kharagpur, India.

I thought it could happen to others but never to me. I was the lead bomber pilot on the first B-29 Superfortress bombing raid on the Japanese home islands and survived many subsequent bombing missions against those same islands. While bombing those islands, I witnessed the first reported kamikaze fighter attacks against B-29s that sent two B-29s and 22 crew members to earth. All were members of my squadron, and I would never see them again. Death was no stranger, but it had never come this close before.

I spoke into the interphone. "Pilot to crew: Prepare to bail out. Open emergency exit doors."

I shouted to Billings, "Colonel, can you get to the escape hatch?"

"I can make it," Billings yelled back and pulled himself up on his undamaged leg.

As I flipped the nose wheel switch, Billings turned to Saltzman and shouted, "Saltzman, open the escape hatch!"

Remembering our briefing instructions, I said, "Pilot to crew: I'm turning to fly over land so we can bail out into the jungle rather than the sea. Left gunner, acknowledge when everyone in the rear is ready to jump."

"Left gunner to pilot: Roger."

"Right gunner to pilot: The fire is coming up through the top of the wing."

"Left gunner to pilot: All crew members in the rear are ready to jump at the rear door."

"Pilot to left gunner: We are over roads and villages. Can we wait a few minutes before bailing out?"

"Left gunner to pilot: I'll go back to the right gunner's blister and look."

Gillett clicked off the interphone. In a few seconds, he came back on. "Left gunner to pilot: The fire is terrible. It is streaming past the tail. We should bail out NOW!"

I could not see the number three engine. I yelled into the interphone, "Be ready to go in case the wing blows off before I give the order to bail out."

Then whoosh! The wing broke off with nothing more than a soft explosion, flipping the plane over onto its side. The crew started jumping.

Saltzman rolled off his seat behind Billings and jumped feet-first down through the open nose wheel escape hatch behind the pilots. Duffy crawled up from the bombardier's seat past Billings and me, bounced back and forth in the tumbling plane, and then took a tumble head-first down the hatch. Hansman and Billings went down the opening one after the other as the plane careened.

When Saltzman jumped down through the escape hatch, the plane turned, and he emerged, not in the cold open air but in a wall of burning gasoline from the right-wing tanks. He covered his face with his hands. The burning fuel seared his face, leaving the imprint of his hands and scorching the rest of his face and ears. The backs of his hands, burnt to the bone, took the brunt of the burning fuel and made them difficult to move. When his flight suit pant legs flew up in the wind above his boot tops, the fire also seared his ankles. Jumping through the flames and tumbling through the air, he somehow pulled his ripcord.

A few minutes later, he crashed down through the top of a tree. His parachute formed a canopy over the top branches and its shroud enveloped him as he swung in his harness 80 feet in the air. After catching his breath and trying to ignore the intense pain, he reached up to grab a branch and swung over to a crotch in the tree. Releasing his chute harness and encircling the tree trunk with just his arms and legs to avoid using his burnt hands, Saltzman slid down the trunk of the tree. About 30 feet from the ground, he could feel his strength ebbing and lost his grip. In desperation, he interlocked his fingers to keep from falling. He felt a sharp pain on the back of his left hand as the fingers of his right hand gouged his burnt flesh. Losing his grasp, Saltzman slid down the trunk, slammed into the ground, and fell backward, banging his head on a tree stump. He laid half-conscious on the ground for several minutes before realizing his surroundings. When awake, he saw his right hand held a fistful of flesh from the back of his left hand.

Lying under the tree, he tried to compose himself. For the moment, his mind was still half blank. He remembered bailing out, but he could not piece together what happened after that. Winded and in pain, Saltzman sat under the tree for a few minutes. He then attempted to patch himself up with the first aid kit he took from his jungle pack. With his eyes almost swollen shut, he couldn't see as he fumbled with the bandages for several minutes with no success. Saltzman could still see well enough to notice all the burnt flesh pulled away from the back of his hand. After deciding to give up on his hands, he stumbled to his feet to begin a hopeful search for his fellow crew members.

Hansman and I had landed just half a mile away, but nobody knew where anyone else was at that point. The gloom deepened as Saltzman trudged along, unable to see more than a few yards ahead. He thought about how the briefings failed to teach the pure reality of survival in the jungle. Few people have an accurate idea of what it is like to be in the Malayan rainforest.

Being alone and reeling in pain from his injuries left Saltzman horrified. He wondered where the rest of the crew landed and was still unaware that Hansman and I were nearby. He hoped the others survived and were not suffering in pain from burns like he was. As he looked at the thick jungle around him, he remembered the knife in his survival kit. Then reality surfaced. Though he carried an Army-issued knife capable of cutting through some tangled vegetation of the thick jungle, his hands were skinless with the burnt flesh pulled away to where he could see his bones and tendons and useless. He thought to himself, "What a predicament for me to be in."

At that moment, Saltzman was not sure if he could endure his situation. But as he pushed ahead, hoping to find other survivors, he hoped that none of them were suffering from the amount of pain he was enduring. After taking a few steps, he stopped when he saw a giant snake a few feet away, hidden in the brush, coiled up awaiting its prey. Saltzman stepped back about six feet into the undergrowth. He stood and stared at the snake, wondering what would happen next. The snake's head must have been two feet above the ground, its body as thick as a telephone pole. To Saltzman's relief, as he watched the snake, it uncoiled itself like a spring and glided away into the darkness of the jungle. Saltzman was sure it was a python and estimated that it measured somewhere between 20 and 30 feet long. He looked around for a second or two and walked on. Every step caused his head to throb, making him feel nauseous. He had a confused mind, and he hoped he did not have a concussion or worse. On top of it all, he had no idea where he was going, but he kept moving on, hoping to find a member of his crew.

When Saltzman had jumped through the plane's open hatch, Duffy had already released his seat belt to bail out. When the *Postville Express* lost her wing, she hurled Duffy sideways to the floor. He grabbed the bottom of the co-pilot's seat with both hands, trying to steady himself in the gyrating B-29 now descending in the air. Duffy pulled himself back up and headed for the escape hatch. Crawling on his hands and knees, he caught a glimpse of me unfastening my seat belt and saw Saltzman jump through the open hatch. When Duffy reached the edge of the escape opening, the plane pitched sideways, throwing him against the wall. When the B-29 turned again, it released Duffy from the wall, and he crawled back to the escape hatch opening. He jumped just as the plane flipped over again, slamming him against the edge of the escape hatch. He felt a sharp pain on his left side when he hit the jagged edge. Then he dropped through the nose wheel hatch, out of the plane and into the air.

After waiting a moment to clear the falling plane, Duffy pulled his ripcord. He was relieved to see his parachute stream out above him. When the chute snapped open, the sudden midair stop wrenched Duffy's side and caused him to cry out with a loud "Damn!"

As Duffy floated to earth, he moved his arms and legs back and forth, checking to see if they still worked. He was glad everything was functioning. Duffy wanted to make sure he could run when his feet hit the ground because he did not know if the natives scurrying around below were friendly or not. As he came closer to landing, he could see one native holding a large bolo knife in his hand and starting to move in his direction.

After Duffy landed in a large clearing at the edge of the jungle, he gathered up his parachute while keeping a close eye on the group of natives and the young Malay running toward him with the big knife. Dropping the chute, Duffy pulled his .45 caliber pistol and pointed it at the young native who came to an abrupt halt 10 feet away. The young man pointed to the parachute lying on the ground, held out his hand palm up, and smiled. It dawned on Duffy that all the young man wanted was the parachute. Duffy tried to speak to him with no success. Putting his gun away, Duffy made a friendly gesture toward the parachute. The young man grabbed the chute and disappeared into the jungle.

Exhausted, Duffy sat on the ground in the shade of a large tree at the edge of the jungle to ponder his situation, gather himself, and rest a few minutes. He heard a startling noise that caused him to jump to his feet. He pulled out his .45 and grabbed his side with the other hand. Something was thrashing around in the jungle brush right behind him. When Duffy stepped back a few feet for a better look, it surprised him to see Lindley appear out of the trees.

Lindley staggered up to Duffy and then slumped down beneath the tree without uttering a word. He appeared to be in a daze. It was clear to Duffy that the flames from the plane had burned Lindley's body when he bailed out.

"Lindley, thank God we found each other! Can you talk?" When Lindley did not answer, Duffy became concerned. "Don't go to sleep. We cannot stay here. We need to keep moving." But the exhausted and burnt Lindley had already dozed off.

Meanwhile, as Saltzman staggered through the jungle, he realized the thick growth was thinning out a bit. Something stopped him in his tracks. Did he hear some voices, or was it his imagination?

Ahead, he could see what appeared to be a clearing through the trees and vines. As he crept up to the opening, it relieved him to see Duffy and Lindley sitting under a tree at the edge of the clearing.

"Thank God!" Saltzman exclaimed. "I never thought I would see you bastards again." As Saltzman sank to sit beside them, he asked, "Have you seen any of the other guys? Did they make it?"

"Boy! It's good to see you, Saltzman!" Duffy replied. "We haven't seen a soul. But maybe the others will show up soon. Let's hope so. Lindley's in no shape to travel, and I may have broken a rib. It hurts to breathe. You don't look so good yourself. Your hands look terrible, Saltz!"

Saltzman looked down at his charred and shivering hands and said, "My ankles are bad, too. I am having a hard time walking. My entire body feels like it's on fire."

As they were talking, another Malay native emerged from the nearby jungle and was approaching them. He appeared to be even younger than the one who took Duffy's chute. The boy pointed toward an animal trail, saying in his best English, "You come. Others that way."

Saltzman and Duffy looked at each other, wondering what he meant by "others."

Duffy imitated an airplane with his arms and said, "Airplane?" The boy nodded his head up and down and said, "Come."

"What are we sitting here for?" Saltzman exclaimed. "Let's go!" When Saltzman grabbed his jungle kit, his burnt hands gave him a jolt of sharp pain, causing him to drop the kit and cry out, "Damn, that hurt!" Then he hauled himself to his feet, still grimacing with pain.

Duffy reached over to shake the dozing Lindley. "Wake up! We need to leave this area. Can you get up okay? We will walk slow. Come on. You can do it."

Lindley looked around at the others through his swollen eyes and said, "Okay, let's go."

Then, with Duffy's help, he rose to his feet. After Duffy grabbed Saltzman's jungle kit, the three of them followed the native Malay boy into the jungle. The bedraggled Airmen followed him around 200 yards on a jungle trail when the boy stopped and pointed at something in the trees. Half hidden by the underbrush lay a parachute harness, a jungle escape pack, and a rubber life vest.

Duffy bent over to pull them out into the open. "They're Hansman's!" Saltzman exclaimed. "Look! His name is on them. The damn Japs got him. The bastards! They've captured him!"

After Duffy saw Hansman's chute and Hansman was nowhere in sight, he started thinking the boy could lead them into a trap. He might lead them right to the Japs. Duffy turned around and placed his forefinger over his lips to signal everybody to be quiet. He turned back around to grab the young Malay, but the boy was gone. He had already melted into the jungle.

Out of sorts, the three American Airmen hesitated for a few minutes, looking at one another, now unsure of their next move.

Duffy glanced both ways along the trail and whispered, "I don't like the looks of this, but we sure as hell can't go back to the plane. Let's stick with the trail."

Saltzman agreed. "Yeah, we have to keep moving. Let's hope we don't bump into any Jap patrols along the way. Be ready to dive into the underbrush if we do."

With that, the trio headed down a narrow animal trail, Duffy in the lead with Lindley and Saltzman following behind. After walking less than a mile, they came on another clearing that looked like it was once part of the jungle but had been cleared off to be a farm. The area was extensive, 150 yards across and about a quarter of a mile long, surrounded with tall jungle trees. There was nothing but thick, dead grass about four feet high in the cleared area.

As they looked around, the far side of the clearing drew their attention. No one could speak for a few moments. Everyone stood there in silence, gazing upon the burning fuselage of a plane.

"It's our plane!" Saltzman exclaimed. "It's the *Postville Express*! I wonder if everyone got out. It's a mess."

The three astonished men looked at their B-29's main fuselage without wings, engines, or tail, burning with 20-foot flames and black smoke filling the air above the wreckage. About 30 curious Malay natives wearing mismatched clothes were standing in the area around the remains of the burning *Postville Express*. One native wore a bright yellow silk shirt. Another Malay wore a white suit, and some others wore mismatched, nondescript clothing. This curious group was the American Airmen's first introduction to the new Malay native culture they would come to know so well.

Duffy said, "Yup, that's her alright. The end of the road for the *Postville Express*."

Lindley said, "I hope everybody made it" and then sat down and passed out.

As Saltzman looked around, he said, "Do you see those guys over there with rifles? It looks like there's about half a dozen of them."

"Yeah, you're right," Duffy replied. "But they look ragtag. They sure don't look like Japs.

"No, they don't," Saltzman answered. "They haven't seen us yet. Maybe we should hightail it out of here before they do."

"Too late. See that guy pointing over here?" Duffy said. "Anyway, we can't leave now with Lindley the way he is." Glancing down at Lindley lying on the ground, Duffy added, "What do you say we try to get the submachine gun out of the plane. We sure as hell could use it."

Saltzman gave Duffy a doubtful look and said, "Hell no! You and me against all those guys with rifles? Are you crazy? Our .45s would be like pop guns against those rifles and whatever else they might have. We would never make it across the field."

"Yeah, maybe. But I still think we are going to need that damn zip gun. You never know. Maybe those people are friendly," Duffy replied.

"Maybe," Saltzman answered. "But we may not live long enough to find out."

"Okay," Duffy said. "But what do you suggest we do now? Go back into the jungle? We have to do something fast."

Undecided, they both pondered their next move as they looked back in the burning plane's direction at the multitude of natives, all now staring back at them.

"Listen." Saltzman pointed toward the jungle behind them. "I hear someone coming."

Leaving Lindley hidden in the tall grass, Saltzman and Duffy ducked into the nearby dense brush. Crouched, with guns drawn, they peered through the thick growth. Two figures emerged from the jungle, not 50 feet away. Saltzman yelled, "Don't shoot, Duff! It's Hump and Hansman."

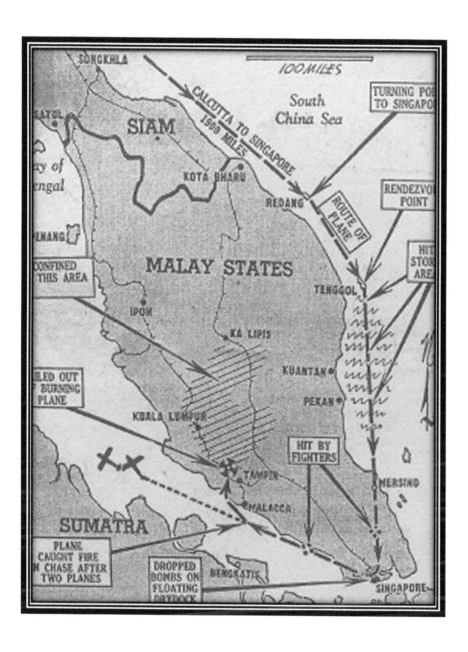

CHAPTER 2

My Jump

Saltzman, Duffy, Billings, and Hansman had already jumped through the escape hatch, and I had just unbuckled my seat belt. I turned around to check the plane, and it looked empty. I never saw Kundrat, who should have been one of the first ones out because he was already sitting next to the escape hatch when the wing blew off.

As the plane somersaulted out of control, it threw me out of my seat and rolled me along the floor toward the escape hatch. I dove through the hatch opening but floated back up into the plane. The centrifugal force flung me against the bulletproof glass in front of the pilots' compartment and pinned me there. The cartwheeling plane then turned over and threw me back against the instrument panel. As the *Postville Express* plunged to earth, the centrifugal force continued to pin me against the instrument panel, and I could not move. As I strained to free myself, the plane took another turn that released me from the instrument panel and allowed me to climb through the escape hatch.

Now out of the plane and falling in cold air, I yanked on the ripcord of my parachute, but nothing happened. Desperate, I gave the ripcord a hard do-or-die yank, and I came to what felt like a jolting stop at 4,000 feet above the ground. I looked down to see if my brand-new paratrooper boots were still on my feet after the sudden jolt. They were. I looked up, puzzled to see several parachutes floating above me. Then I realized I had ridden in the fast-falling plane past the other chutes while attempting to get out.

What grabbed my attention, however, was the *Postville Express*. I could not take my eyes off her as the wounded bomber twisted and turned, hurtling to earth like a flaming meteorite. With only one wing, the stress on the plummeting B-29 was too severe, and she disintegrated. The other wing broke off. Next came the engines breaking away, and then the fuselage snapped in two.

As I swung in my parachute harness on the way down, something startled me. I flinched when I saw out of the corner of my eye what I thought was a Jap fighter flashing by. After it passed, I twisted around to take a better look behind me. I saw it was the *Postville Express*'s tail section with its 468th Bomber Group red stripes—my plane's last farewell.

Watching this was a poignant moment for me. The *Postville Express* was not just a plane to me. I had the honor of naming her the *Postville Express* after my hometown of Postville, Iowa, which also made this a personal loss.

As I bid a silent goodbye to the *Postville Express*, I heard someone yell, "Hump!" Looking in the direction of the shout, I saw Carl Hansman, the navigator, floating down nearby.

I yelled back, "You alright, Hansman?"

"Yeah, I'm still in one piece. How about you?"

"Banged up a bit, but okay," I answered.

"See a suitable spot to land, Hump?" Hansman yelled back.

"How about that clearing near the rice fields?" I said, pointing in that direction.

"Looks good to me," Hansman shouted. "Who are those natives down there?"

I glanced at the fast-approaching ground and yelled, "Beats me! But I don't see any Japs."

Having misjudged our altitude, wind, and airspeed, I realized the wind current now pushed us toward the tall trees. Missing the jungle clearing altogether, I ended up crashing through the top of a 150-foot tree. It was a typical Malayan jungle hardwood tree with its lowest branches about 100 feet above the ground.

With my parachute entangled in the upper limbs, I hung in the air at the height of an eight-story building. I tugged on the parachute shrouds to ensure the silk parachute would not slip down through the branches. I pulled myself up hand-over-hand to reach the branches above. After hoisting myself up several feet, I slid back down and became too exhausted and sweaty to continue. After resting a few minutes, I tried it again and quit when I realized I did not have the strength to do it. Although it was still early in the morning, the Malayan rainforest was steaming. This area where we crashed was less than 100 miles from the equator, and it was hot.

I tried to swing back and forth to grab onto the trunk of the enormous tree I was hanging in, but that did not work. I panicked, thinking the Japs could show up and shoot me like a trapped bird as I dangled in my harness.

Someone yelled, "Hump, where are you?"

Because I was in the middle of Japanese-occupied territory, I hesitated to yell back and give away my location to the Japs.

"Hump! It's me, Hansman. You okay?"

"Yeah! I'm caught up here in a tree," I shouted back.

"Hold on! I'll be right there," he answered.

After what seemed like a long time, I saw Hansman appear at the foot of the tree. He looked tiny from my view 100 feet above the ground. I did not realize I was so high off the ground until I saw how minuscule Hansman looked. I was thankful I did not succumb to my first impulse to cut myself loose and drop to the ground. That would have been the drop of death.

"I'm glad to see you. Can you get me down from here?" I yelled.

I knew I needed to get down as fast as possible. The Japanese Occupation Army controlled this area with many troops. There was no way they could miss seeing the *Postville Express* falling and burning in the sky and the crew's parachutes floating down. I knew these troops would soon pinpoint our location and look for us.

Hansman sized up the situation and tried climbing the tree. But the trunk was six feet in diameter and much too smooth to get a grip. "No way I can climb this baby," Hansman shouted. "Maybe I can figure something out." Hansman stepped back some distance from the tree and pondered the problem. "I wish I had something to work with to get you down, Hump. But looking around here in the jungle, I don't see any ropes or ladders anywhere handy," he said with a laugh.

Hansman continued to contemplate the situation. As he glanced around, he noticed a nearby tree about 70 feet tall. He thought it might have branches that could reach my tree about 25 feet away.

"Hump, if I get a knife up to you, can you cut off a few of your parachute shrouds long enough to reach that tree over there?"

"Yeah, I think so," I replied.

Hansman jumped up to grab one of the smaller tree's lower branches and hoisted himself into the lower part of the tree. He climbed until he reached a height where he was a few feet lower than me.

"Here, catch," Hansman said as he tossed me his Army knife. It was a perfect toss. I caught the knife while hanging mid-air.

"Good catch!" Hansman shouted.

"Thanks! So far, so good," I answered. Then I cut off two of the shrouds and tied them together to make a rope about 30 feet long.

Hansman yelled, "Tie one end of the shrouds to your chute harness, and throw the other end to me."

After tying one end of the make-shift rope to the chute harness, I tossed the other end to Hansman. He tied his end of the shroud to his tree so it sloped down from me.

"Now, grab onto the shroud as you get out of your harness," Hansman yelled.

"Say a prayer this will hold!" I shouted as I released my harness.

The chute harness and make-shift rope combination dipped down as I hung on for dear life. With my heart pounding out of my chest, I threw one leg over the make-shift rope and slid down toward the other tree.

Reaching the tree, I gasped for a breath. "You pulled it off, Hansman. I thought I would be up there forever. Now, let's get the hell out of this tree. We are already stretching our luck staying around here this long. It has been at least an hour. I'm surprised the Japs haven't found us by now."

"Yeah, let's go," Hansman replied. "I wonder what happened to the other guys."

"I don't know. Let's see if we can find them," I answered.

We climbed down the tree with no other words said, dropped to the ground, and headed for the underbrush. We started down a jungle trail, not knowing if we were going in the right direction but hoping to find some other crew members. As the path opened into a clearing, we heard an unexpected shout that stopped us in our tracks. I could not believe my eyes when I saw Duffy and Saltzman step out of the jungle with their big smiles.

"You made it!" Saltzman exclaimed. "We thought we would never see you guys again!"

Saltzman pointed toward the high brown grass and said, "Hump, Lindley's right over there. In terrible shape, too."

As I went over to check on Lindley's condition, Hansman exclaimed, "Wow! Is that the *Postville Express?*"

I turned to see the burning wreckage across the open field and knew it was the *Postville Express*. I named and nurtured that plane. We flew many missions together. It felt like there was a piece of me dying in those flames along with her.

Duffy, Saltzman, Hansman, and I were in somewhat of a daze. We stood around the semi-conscious Ralph Lindley lying on the ground and surmised the scene on the opposite side of the jungle clearing.

Duffy said, "Hump, those fellows with the guns could be some local native militia the way they're surrounding the plane with so much curiosity."

Saltzman remarked, "You would not believe it, Hump. Duff wants to go across the field to sneak the zip gun out of the burning plane. I think he's crazy!"

I settled that matter. "We're not going over there. Come on, let's get Lindley on his feet and get out of here."

Hansman and Duffy roused Lindley and helped him up. Hansman said in a low voice, "Lindley, we'll carry you. We must get moving. The Japs could spot us here. They may be along any second."

Lindley took a few slow steps and then murmured through his swollen lips, "Don't worry about me. I will make it. Let's go."

Hearing that, I waded through the high grass toward the jungle. The others followed. We only walked a few yards when I saw two Malay natives come out of the jungle dead ahead of me, walking toward us. We could see the tops of their heads just above the five-foot-tall grass.

I slowed down and said in a low voice, "Keep your guns ready but out of sight. Take safeties off."

There was no place to hide, so I just stopped. The leading Malay native was a short, maybe five-foot-tall male wearing trousers that were too small, a shirt much too large, and what appeared to be a lady's cast-off bolero jacket. On his head was a mangled brown velvet fez, the kind Shriners wear in the United States. Behind him was a younger Malay boy dressed in what looked like a white cotton nightgown.

We eyed the two natives. I wondered why they were approaching us. I was in no frame of mind to trust anyone. We were lucky so far, and I wanted to keep it that way. I did not know if these fellows were friendly or not. All I knew for sure was that if they were not and if we were going to die, these two guys were going with us.

My anxiety diminished as the natives drew closer. They did not appear armed or dangerous and were altogether comical looking. We did not scare the Malay natives, even though we were much taller than they were and armed. The older native kept his eyes fixed on me. Not once did he glance at the four other haggard men standing behind me. Then he rushed through the grass and came to a halt in front of me, about two feet away. He removed his velvet fez and bowed. As he straightened up, his wrinkled brown face creased into a big smile. "Good morning, Tuan," he said with an Oxford accent.

We could not hide our surprise. We all laughed a laugh of relief. This little Malay man looked like an organ grinder's monkey, but he spoke English like Winston Churchill. From the expressions on our faces and laughter, he realized we did not expect his formal greeting. Looking up at me, the smiling little man appeared to be happy with his performance. The younger Malay stood behind him with a big grin on his face.

I hesitated before replying while I looked over the Malay natives across the clearing. These two in front of me seemed harmless. They also appeared to be unarmed, which was another good sign. However, the armed natives still gathered around the remains of the *Postville Express*'s burning wreckage were staring in our direction and looked like they could be trouble. The flight's briefing officer had warned against trusting the Malay natives if we were shot down because many of them worked for the Japanese and loved the reward money.

Taking another glance at the armed men across the clearing, I knew time was of the essence and responded, "Good morning. We are Americans. We need your help. Can you hide us from the Japanese?"

The Malay man looked up at me, smiling, and pointed toward the young boy behind him. "This is my son. Yes, we will help you. Please, come with us."

Hearing his enthusiastic yes, we all followed the Malay native and his son. But after only a few steps, Duffy said, "I don't know. These guys could be anybody."

Everybody stopped and stood there looking at each other. After reassuring ourselves that the Malay natives were our best bet, we started down the path again and followed the Malay native and the boy.

Duffy, though, having some doubts, jumped a few steps ahead of us, turned around, and said, "I think we would be crazy to follow this guy. Where is he taking us? To the Japs? Maybe we would be better off on our own. What do you think?"

Hansman replied, "You may be right, but I don't like the looks of the jungle, either. Where would we go once we got in there?"

Saltzman glanced at the disappearing natives, looked at the dense jungle, and asked, "Hump, what do you think? It's your call."

"Let's stick with these two guys," I replied. "They are leading us in the right direction, away from the plane, and they are unarmed and seem to be friendly. They speak English, or at least the older one does. Stay alert and keep your .45s ready in case there's trouble. The important thing now is to move as far away from the crash site as possible, as fast as possible. I'm mighty surprised we haven't already seen some Japs in this area."

I started walking to catch up with the two natives, and the others followed behind me. We walked for several minutes on an animal path when the jungle closed around us. As I followed behind the Malay father, he turned to talk to me. Speaking over his shoulder, he said, "My name is Talib. I am the Headman of Kampong Kota. The Japanese are closing in on this area. We must hurry because I am sure they saw your plane come down. They know I am Headman in this area, so they will look for me also to find out what I know."

"We thank you for helping us," I replied. "My name is Major Humphrey. I was the pilot of the plane. If your people locate any other members of our crew, please bring them to me."

Talib answered in his clipped English, "I do not know of any others. If we find others, we will bring them."

Hansman, behind me, asked in a low voice, "Who were those guys with the guns back at the crash site?"

Talib replied, "They are Malay troops recruited by the Japanese. They serve as police forces in rural areas. It is wise to avoid them."

Duffy interjected, "How many Japs are near here?"

Talib responded, "About 300 stationed at Tampin, a village only six miles away. There are 500 more at Seremban, 15 miles in the other direction."

"How fast can they get here?" I asked.

Talib answered, "Quick. A concrete road and a railroad are connecting the two villages. The road passes only two miles from the plane crash. The Japanese are close to us already. If my son yells out, leave the trail fast and hide in the underbrush. No noise."

Lindley and Saltzman had the most difficulty keeping up with the pace. Both were in agony from their burns. Lindley stared straight ahead as he plodded along with robot-like movements. Saltzman's lower legs and ankles were raspberry red and swollen. Every step was pure hell. Hansman dropped back to bring up the rear and monitor them.

"How much farther do we have to go?" Saltzman moaned. "Can we take a break?"

"No!" replied Talib. "We must clear out of this area fast before they track us. I do not trust some people back at the wreck. The Japanese promised a $10,000 reward to anyone who turns in a downed enemy flyer. It is more money than any of them will see in a lifetime."

After two hours of fast walking, Talib and his son veered off the trail and led us into a small hidden ravine. The gorge was five feet deep with sloped sides. This hiding place looked like it would do an excellent job of concealing us with its tall, dense jungle brush. It was only a few feet off the trail, but the thick brush would cover us well.

As we all dropped to the ground, Talib instructed us in a low voice, "Lie down here and rest. Be quiet. Do not move around. There could be hundreds of troops moving along this trail. I will be back at midnight."

To our surprise, he whistled a tune and said, "I will whistle this tune when I return at midnight. When you hear it, come out on the trail to meet me. I will try to take you where some Australian and British soldiers live in the jungle."

Talib then gave us another quick rendition of the tune, turned, and hurried out of the ravine, leaving us in our jungle refuge.

CHAPTER 3

Talib

I t was now early afternoon. The Malayan rainforest was hot and steaming with humidity. The short trees, the dense vines, and the underbrush locked in the smoldering, moist heat. We felt confined, hot, and cramped in the small ravine surrounded by thick, green jungle growth. We were thankful for a secure place to hide because the Japanese Army also surrounded our location. As we entrenched ourselves in our hideout, we could not help but notice the eerie afternoon silence that settled upon the jungle. No leaves were rustling, no birds were singing, and no wildlife was stirring. All was silent.

We could settle down together to semi-relax a bit for the first time since the five of us met up at the clearing near the plane crash. As I looked around, I noticed how close we were to the trail and whispered, "We will need some warning if there is any movement on the trail, so we will have to rotate watches. Everyone stay alert and keep your voices down. Does anyone want the first watch?"

Duffy whispered, "Those yellow bastards must be all over the place looking for us. My side is aching so bad it's hard to move, but I can still stand watch, Hump."

"Okay, Duff," I replied, "You take the first watch. Keep a sharp eye on the trail in both directions."

"Okay," Duffy said, "But first, tell me this. Does anyone know whether the rest of the crew made it?"

Saltzman replied, "I saw several chutes on the way down scattered all over the place. I could not tell who they were. You guys are the only ones I know about."

I nodded in agreement. "Hard to figure out who got out of the rear section. Maybe Lindley can shed some light on it when he is up to it. Let's hope they all got out."

"Hump, what happened to Kundrat?" Hansman asked. "When we were talking one day, he told me he would never jump out of an airplane. Did he go down with the plane?"

"I was the last one out," I replied. "I saw no sign of him. He must have jumped."

Just before Duffy moved into his lookout position, the faint sound of voices broke the stillness. The voices grew louder and louder from what appeared to be a patrol of Japanese troops approaching and headed in the direction of the crash.

We were five exhausted and bedraggled American Airmen who were still very aware of our vulnerable and dangerous circumstances. We crouched down, pressing our bodies into the ground, and hoped to avoid detection.

I drew my .45 and signaled to the others to do the same. As I held my gun at the ready, I lifted my head to peer through the underbrush. I could see several pairs of shoes and leggings striding past only a dozen feet away. They were too close for comfort. Because of the quietness of the jungle, I knew our slightest sound would alert them and result in a deadly barrage of gunfire into our narrow ravine. I was also afraid Lindley might cry out in pain as he did from time to time. Only after the sound of the Japanese soldiers' voices and stomping feet faded did we breathe a collective sigh of relief.

After the patrol passed, the jungle trail was quiet again. Saltzman tugged on my shirtsleeve and whispered, "My hands and ankles are killing me. Look at these ankles, Hump. They're a mess, and they are driving me crazy."

When I pulled up the pant legs of Saltzman's flight suit, I winced when I saw how burnt and swollen his right ankle appeared. The left one seemed in better shape than the right. Reaching for my Army knife, I said in a low voice, "Your right ankle has swelled up so much that your boot top is cutting into it. There is not much I can do, but I will cut off the top of your boot and put some sulfa powder on the worst burnt areas. Then maybe you'll be able to walk a little better."

"Okay," Saltzman replied, "But take it easy. It hurts like hell."

After cutting the boot top away, I sprinkled some sulfa powder on the raw flesh and applied a bandage. Then I turned my attention to Saltzman's hands. Looking at the exposed tendons, I whispered, "They look awful. Can you move your fingers?"

"Yeah," Saltzman replied. "They're killing me, but I guess I can use them."

"I'll put some of this sulfa powder on them."

"No, don't!" Saltzman shouted. "We just have just a few sulfa packets left. We may need it later. Besides, my dad always said, 'Let nature take its course.'"

"Shh! Keep your voice down, Saltz. We might have an unknown visitor close by."

Checking on Saltzman's burnt face and ears, I whispered. "I wish I could do more, but I guess that's about it for now."

Saltzman nodded in silent agreement.

Next, I looked at Lindley, who appeared to be in a state of shock. He slept most of the time lying flat on his back. Whenever he moved in his sleep, he moaned with pain. "How are you doing?" I asked as I knelt close beside him.

Never one to complain, Lindley mumbled through his swollen, burnt lips, "Okay, I guess."

I whispered, "Lindley, I know it hurts to talk, but you're the only one here who was at the plane's rear exit. Did everyone get out?"

"Can't say for sure," Lindley muttered. "When you gave the order to prepare to bail out, I left my gun and headed for the emergency exit. MacDonald, Gillett, and Govednik were already there, ready to jump. I could see Spratt coming up from the tail as the flames shot by the exit door from number three. When the wing blew off, we all went sprawling all over the place, throwing me away from the exit door, but I crawled my way back. When Spratt went out the exit door, I went right behind him. We both jumped right into those damn flames. God, it burned! I couldn't see anything, so I didn't see if any of the other guys jumped. Thank God, my chute still worked. I don't remember much after that."

Lindley's face, ears, and hands were red and raw from the burns, and he could not open his eyes. He was in agony.

I applied sulfa powder to the burns and said, "We are trying to find you some help, Lindley. You need hospital care. Hang in there. We will get out of this mess."

Lindley raised his right hand, gave me the victory sign, and dozed off again. I prayed that what I just told Lindley would happen.

Watching this, Hansman interjected, "Hump, why don't we give Lindley and Saltzman some morphine? They are hurting bad."

"I don't think we'd better," I replied. "If a Jap patrol spots us, they need to move.

Lindley and Saltzman, both suffering, drifted off to sleep. The afternoon dragged on as Hansman, Duffy, and I took turns on watch. The peaceful atmosphere had a soothing effect on us.

At sunset on our first night in Malaya, the jungle came alive with sounds of every kind. The first sound was a sharp staccato "KAKK" from a bird. It sounded like a repetitive Morse code radio signal, so we named it Radio Bird. This early evening announcement from Radio Bird set off all the other jungle wildlife. The silence that reigned just minutes before became a clamoring chorus of various jungle animal sounds.

While Hansman was on watch, Duffy and I tried to sleep but found it next to impossible because of the jungle din. We were also too jumpy. The chirping insects, squawking birds, croaking frogs, and intermittent grunting sounds of mysterious origin in the surrounding bush proved too much. We were also uneasy because the jungle serenade might mask our chance to hear any approaching Japanese troops on the trail.

Since neither of us could sleep, I whispered, "Duff, before it gets too dark, let's run a check on our gear to see what we have left."

We started with the jungle survival kits attached to our parachute harnesses. We could only find four among the five of us. Each kit contained a knife, matches, fishing gear, a book called *How to Survive in the Jungle,* first aid supplies, Atabrine tablets for malaria, sulfa powder, morphine, halazone pills, mosquito head nets and repellent, an English-Chinese dictionary, a map, a compass, a metal mirror for signaling airplanes, a machete, and an Army-issued Chinese-English Pointie Talkie book.

On each man's web belt were a canteen, an ammunition pouch, a knife, a sheath, a medical kit, and a .45 caliber handgun.

"We're still in good shape," Duffy murmured. "But we could use more medical supplies. We'll use up what we have on Saltzman and Lindley in the next few days."

As I peered through the darkness at Lindley and Saltzman lying passed out beside us, I said, "Yeah, let's pray God helps them. They are in awful shape."

I pulled out my .45 and said, "At least we have our five guns and 140 rounds. We may need them before the night's over. If things happen, Duffy, you better grab Lindley's .45. He's in no shape to use it."

Glancing toward Hansman, I added, "It's dark. I will relieve Hansman now. He can use some shut-eye."

Towering jungle trees blocked the moon, making the trail almost pitch black. Jungle noises smothered any sounds of the Jap patrols approaching on the path. This difficulty in distinguishing the sounds made our situation precarious. Only extreme alertness by the man on watch could prevent our detection and keep us safe.

After relieving Hansman, I glanced down at the luminous dial of my watch and thought, "Ten o'clock. We have placed our bets on Talib. We'll find out in two hours whether he returns alone or with Japs."

Then a sound emanated from the trail. I heard voices. Only a few words, but in Japanese. I crawled over to Duffy and whispered, "Japs. Pass the word."

We drew our .45s and waited. The voices grew louder as the patrol approached, a larger group this time in single file and moving fast on the trail just a few feet above our hidden nest. As we held our breaths, it seemed like an eternity before the last man in the column passed by us.

When I thought the Japs had left, I whispered, "It looks like we bet on the right guy, Duff. I'm sure those guys would have been all over us if Talib already told them about us and our location."

"I sure hope you're right, Hump," Duffy whispered. "But I still don't trust him."

During the next two hours, two smaller patrols passed by our location. We thanked God that it was so dark and the jungle growth was so thick. We had to give Talib credit. He picked the right hiding place.

Stretched out side by side, Duffy and I discussed our predicament in low, hushed voices as the others slept.

"Hump, what do you think? Should we trust this Talib guy?"

I had been asking myself that same question throughout the day.

Turning my head toward Duffy, I said, "If we leave now and try it on our own, the damn Japs will find us and capture us. The trail is full of them. I don't think we have a choice. We need Talib. We cannot find our way around in this jungle without a guide. Besides, Saltzman and Lindley need medical attention. Talib might help us find a doctor."

"But Hump, I wonder why Talib is doing this for us. Is he going to turn us over to the Japs later for a big reward? Do you think there are Australian and British soldiers out there somewhere like he says?"

"What do you think we should do, Duff?"

Hansman, who also could not sleep, listened and jumped in, "This Malay guy does not know us from Adam. What do we mean to him? What would you do if you knew the Nips would shoot you in the head if they caught you hiding American Airmen?"

"Yeah, I've been thinking about that, too," Duffy replied. "But I agree with Hump. We will never get out of this jungle alive without some help from the natives."

Since I was the senior officer present, I ended the discussion by saying, "Our chances are better with Talib, better than in the jungle alone with the Japs everywhere. We'll wait for Talib."

In the minutes just before midnight, we listened and hoped Talib would come back without the Japs. What would we do if he did not come at all?

We thought Lindley was out cold when he sat up and whispered, "That's it, Hump! That's the tune our native friend said he would whistle."

No one else heard a sound.

Then Lindley whispered, "He's here. Let's go!"

Duffy and I climbed up the embankment, parting the dense brush so we could see. There was Talib, right on time at the stroke of midnight with two young Malay boys standing beside him on the trail.

"Come," whispered Talib. "We must move fast. All of you listen. Take off your shoes. The Japs will see your shoe tracks. They're all around here."

We sat down on the ground and took our boots off. Then Duff,

Hansman, and I took the boots off Saltzman and Lindley and tied their bootlaces together. Avoiding the burned areas on their faces, we hung the boots around each of their necks.

After we finished taking off our boots and we all were barefoot, Talib exclaimed in a hushed tone, "Hurry!"

We all followed Talib and the two young boys down the trail in a single file through the pitch-black night. Talib was behind the two boys, and then me, Duffy, Saltzman, and Lindley. Hansman was last in line to monitor Saltzman and Lindley. After walking less than an hour, Talib stopped and motioned for us to sit down. In Malay, he instructed the two boys to go ahead.

He explained to us, "There is a village ahead. The boys will see if the Japanese are there. We may have to go around it."

I asked, "Talib, where are you taking us? Can we get in touch with the Allied Forces?"

Talib replied, "At the moment, I am concerned with avoiding the Japanese patrols. They are everywhere in the area because of the plane crash. We will try to contact the Allies for you when it is safe to do so."

The boys returned and motioned for us to move out. After a few minutes, the jungle thinned out, and a small native village composed of several thatched huts became visible through the trees. We did not see anyone, and no fires were burning anywhere. We walked straight through this quiet village down the trail to the opposite side.

As we reentered the jungle, Saltzman whispered to Duffy, "It looks like somebody warned them to stay in their huts. I think it was for their protection. Now they can say they never saw us."

Duffy nodded his head. "Yeah, I agree, Saltz. Damn, this jungle is dark. I can't see any of you guys. Can't even see the trail!"

I agreed with Duffy. "Yeah, it is difficult to stay on the trail in this dark jungle. Do all of you have a white handkerchief? If you do, try tying it to the back of the person's belt in front of you. That should help you see and follow each other. We don't want to lose anyone."

When I said "lose anyone," we lost someone. We heard a cry of pain coming from somewhere in the dark. It sounded like someone crashing through some underbrush.

A muffled yell followed. "Watch out! I fell into some water! I can't see a thing!" It was Saltzman's voice.

"Where are you, Saltz? Keep talking so we can find you," I said.

"I am down here. Get me out of here!" Saltzman shouted.

"I think I've located you, Saltz. We are on the way," I said, trying to reassure him.

In the pitch-black night, hanging on to trees and vines, Duffy and I worked our way down a steep, 20-foot embankment. We pulled Saltzman out of the bottom of a four-foot deep water-filled ditch. After we rested a minute at the bottom, we all worked our way back up the embankment and helped Saltzman back to the trail. His skinless, burned hands, his burned face, and his burned ankles were all bleeding and covered with black mud. He looked and felt terrible.

We sat beside the trail for several minutes to allow Saltzman to gather himself together and catch his breath. He and Lindley were both in extreme pain and needed a rest. After they rested a bit, Talib instructed his native boys to pull them to their feet again. Saltzman and Lindley fought the pain and kept up even when the pace became faster than before. Talib picked up the pace because he wanted to move us out of the plane crash area as fast as possible. He knew the Japs were everywhere.

The white handkerchiefs helped a bit, and we moved on with limited visibility. The overhead canopy of tree foliage blocked any moonlight. It seemed like we were inside a black box. Walking in single file on paths with rough, uneven terrain and unsure footing made us bump into each other. Walking was painful and exhausting.

Bringing up the rear, Hansman suggested, "Why don't we put a hand on the shoulder of the guy in front of us? Maybe that will work."

Duffy laughed and remarked, "Saltz, I sure as hell don't want to put my hand on your shoulder. I don't swim that well."

It was now 3:00 a.m. on January 12, 1945, the morning of the second day in the jungle. It was sweltering hot. During the day, the sun dissipated the humidity above the high jungle trees. But below, under cover of the tall foliage, the humidity remained high 24 hours a day. It felt like we lived in a continuous steam bath, always sweating. We long ago drank all the water in our canteens, and thirst became a genuine issue. Our mouths were dry, and our throats were parched.

Saltzman murmured, "Damn, I'd give a year's pay for a mug of ice-cold beer."

I commented, "A frosty glass of water would be enough for me right now. But I sure wouldn't turn down a nice cold Budweiser, either."

Lindley was the one most affected by the heat. Exhausted, with a swollen face and eyes, he continued to falter. He stumbled along as best he could as he rambled incoherent words. Dehydrated from a lack of body fluids, he looked like his strength was melting away. He plodded along with the rest of us, exhibiting enormous inner courage. His reputation for never complaining was showing. However, he had reached a point now where each step could be his last.

"Major!" Lindley called out. "I can't go any farther. Leave me here. I don't care. This walking is killing me."

I nodded and said, "Let's take a quick break, fellas, while I give Lindley some of this morphine."

Everybody sprawled on the ground for a few minutes of rest while I tended to Lindley.

"Okay, let's go," I said, and we were back on the trail. But it became a struggle for all of us to keep up with Talib's fast pace. I followed behind Talib and the boys. Saltzman was behind me, and last were Hansman and Duffy, who was supporting Lindley. I knew Lindley and Saltzman could not last much longer, and the others, including me, were not in much better shape. It became difficult to take each step because of dehydration and hunger.

At 3:30 a.m., we walked out of the dark jungle into a flat, moonlit valley terraced with rice paddies. Talib stopped at the edge of the open area and once again sent the boys ahead to scout.

"Very dangerous here to be out in the open," Talib explained. "Japanese may observe any movements in the paddies. The moon is bright, too. Dangerous."

I pulled Talib aside and stated, "I want you to know we intend to resist any Japs who try to take us. We have guns, and we will use them. Talib, you are unarmed. If you want to run away, go ahead. I won't blame you."

Talib thought this over. Then, in his British-flavored accent, he whispered, "We never fight the Japanese with weapons. They have too many troops and arms. The nature of our resistance is different. If you wish to fight them, you may do so, but I think it is better to escape without violence. That way, you will live to fight another day. I am also thinking of my villagers. A fight would bring their deaths and yours."

As I mulled this over, the boys returned and signaled all clear. The 10-minute rest seemed to help restore some of Lindley's energy because he pulled himself to his feet without help and moved out with the rest of us.

Once in the rice paddies, we filled our canteens with field water and dropped in a halazone pill to purify it. Being so dehydrated, we found it difficult to wait the required 15 minutes for the halazone to work, but we followed the directions and held off for the prescribed amount of time before we drank.

After drinking the muddy water, we felt somewhat revived. As we started crossing the several miles of rice paddies, we knew we needed to pick up our pace the best we could to get out of the moonlit view of the Japs. We moved fast without stopping or slowing down to fill our canteens along the way. We reached the far side and found our water containers drained dry. Because of the fast trip across, all of us were dehydrated. Standing at the edge of the rice paddies, we refilled our canteens and dropped in the halazone purifying pills. This time, however, because of our extreme thirst, nobody waited the prescribed 15 minutes and gulped the water down like thirsty hound dogs and risked deadly infections and diarrhea.

At 4:00 a.m. as we were reentering the darkness of the Malayan jungle, I glanced back just before turning to go down the path. I stopped and stood for a minute to admire the magnificent beauty of the rice fields sparkling in the moonlight. It was a sight to see, one I will not forget.

Fatigue slowed our pace as we plodded along behind Talib and the two boys. I sensed the crew's weariness. Stunned and also impressed by our Malay guide's endurance, I said to Talib, "We can't go much farther without rest. My men are exhausted with this fast pace, and I think it's time we pulled off the trail to get some sleep."

Talib, not breaking his stride, turned his head and replied, "Please persevere. We are almost there. In a few more minutes, you will eat and sleep."

Talib was right, at least about the eating part. In just a few minutes, we came to a small native basha buried deep in the bush. With no hesitation, Talib pulled back the burlap bag at the entry door and went in. Then he invited us to enter the small hut.

Talib shouted, "Siap makanan! Lekas!" (Get food! Quick!) He woke up an older Chinese woman sleeping on the floor in the corner. The woman, in her late 50s, jumped to her feet and disappeared into another room. She soon returned with several bowls of cooked rice in hand. We sat on the floor of this filthy, roach-filled, two-room grass hut and stuffed down our rice, trying to satisfy our hunger.

As we sat on the floor eating our rice, with no warning, out of nowhere, and without a sound, two young Chinese showed up at the basha entrance. A young man around 20 years old dressed in khaki shorts, a bright green button-down shirt, and no shoes came in first through the burlap-covered entrance door. Then a pretty, young Chinese girl around 18 years old with shiny black shoulder-length hair and wearing men's pants rolled up to her calves, a sleeveless shirt, and no shoes followed him in. All eyes, including mine, became fixed on this beautiful young lady. They both greeted Talib in Chinese like they knew one another. It also seemed like the Chinese already knew we were coming to this location for a pre-arranged meeting.

Talib turned to us and said, "I will leave you now. These people will be your guides from now on."

He chatted with the two young Chinese for a few minutes more and then turned to us to introduce the pair. But since he continued speaking in Chinese, it was difficult to understand their names. Along with all the different introductions and departures, there were many bows in all directions.

I said, "Thank you for your help, Talib."

Then Talib grasped me by the hand and exclaimed, "We are in this fight together. With God's help, we will drive the Japanese from our land. I wish you and your men well. May you reunite with your compatriots, Tuan. These two young Chinese do not speak English, but I know you will communicate with them. I only have one request, but it is important. If the Japanese capture you, do not give them my name. It would cause my death and those in my village."

Upon saying that, he turned and walked out of the hut.

CHAPTER 4

George and Georgette

Much to our dismay, our two new guides showed us it was time to leave. Still not rested, we left what remained of our rice and followed the two young Chinese out of the hut back into the jungle.

The young man led, and the girl followed close behind him, lugging a massive bundle of clothing on her shoulders. The rest of us followed her.

Duffy, walking alongside me, whispered, "Damn, we were just getting used to Talib, and now we're in the hands of these two. I hope they know where they're going."

I replied, "Once again, we have no choice. We are never getting out of this jungle without help. Did you catch their names?"

Duffy answered, "No. Talib introduced them too fast, and he was speaking in Chinese. I did not understand what he said."

Saltzman interrupted, "You all know what we called our automatic pilot, and this guy is our automatic pilot now. So let's call him George."

Hansman added with a smile, "If we're going to name him George, let's call the girl Georgette."

We later discovered his Chinese name was Wong Kwang, and her Chinese name was Liew Siew Yeng. But for the duration of our time together, wayfaring through the jungle, they were George and Georgette to us.

Since the crash, it seemed as if we were on what I would consider an autopilot trek through the jungle. First, I allowed Talib to guide us without knowing where he was taking us. And now, I let our new autopilots lead us wherever they thought we should go. We meandered on our path, respecting whatever our native guides suggested we do. I was okay with this so far. I hoped by following these natives I was doing the right thing to get us all home safely.

After walking for two hours with our two new Chinese guides, dawn broke, and George wanted to hole up for a while. He led us up to a small clearing on top of a hill in an abandoned and overgrown rubber plantation surrounded by jungle.

We sprawled out on the ground under the trees to rest. Using several gestures with his hands to communicate, George showed us he was leaving to find some food. While we were not sure where he went, he soon returned with a bundle full of dried rice and sweet potatoes, and we prepared for a much-needed meal.

Because of Lindley's burned and swollen lips, opening his mouth to eat was not an easy effort. And Saltzman, who couldn't use his hands, also had a hard time trying to feed himself. Georgette, seeing their need for help, walked over, sat down between the two of them, and with a compassionate smile fed both Lindley and Saltzman as best she could.

It was now 7:00 on the morning of January 12, 1945, still our second day in the jungle. The weather was always humid. Lindley and Saltzman fell asleep after eating. Duffy, Hansman, and I tried to do the same, but George treated us to a lecture. He could not speak English, but his actions spoke for themselves.

George pulled out some Japanese occupation currency, the paper bills the Japanese printed for everybody to use after Japan occupied Malaya. He spat on the bills several times and screamed at them. It was likely he was cursing at them in Chinese. After that, George squatted and pretended to use the paper bills for toilet paper. He jumped back up and grabbed a small book out of his pocket. The book, written in Chinese, had a picture of the Kremlin on the inside front cover, and on the opposite page was a blood-red flag with three golden stars emblazoned on the upper left-hand corner. As George pointed to each star one by one, he smiled and said, "China, India, Malaya." Then he dropped to his knees in front of the group, stared into our eyes, and exclaimed, "Me, Communee! Me, Communee!" He jumped back to his feet, came to attention, and saluted us with a clenched right fist.

His enthusiasm spread to Georgette who also stood to give us an enthusiastic clenched right-fist salute. By gesturing with her hands and using a small dried branch to draw stick figures in the dirt, she tried to tell us her story about how the Japanese murdered her family, killed her husband, and then raped her and left her to die. Georgette also conveyed the idea that this was why she joined the Communists in their war against the Japanese.

At first, George's continued antics amused us until we realized the Chinese pair were serious about their Communist affiliation. After Georgette showed us how she suffered because of the brutal atrocities the Japanese had carried out, we understood even better.

George lectured us, an audience who did not understand a word, but we knew what he was trying to convey. It was our first introduction to the Communist Party in Malaya.

Duffy turned to me and remarked, "I never thought we would travel with two Communists. These two are gung-ho about that Red crap."

I replied, "Yes, it's kind of weird sitting here in the middle of the Malayan jungle listening to a spiel on Communism delivered in

Chinese. Me, I'm going to get some shut-eye."

With that, I stretched out on my back and closed my eyes. But as tired as I was, sleep was slow in coming. My mind was racing. Where are the rest of my crew? Are they alive? Was I leading my men in the right direction to get them home? I believed we were doing the right thing, the only thing possible when you came right down to it. We had eluded the Jap patrols, but now we needed to find a radio transmitter somewhere to contact our Allies—American, British, or Australian, whoever we could reach. Not only could this result in a potential rescue, but our families needed to know we were alive. I could visualize the Missing in Action telegram my parents would receive so soon after the death of my only brother, Howard, killed in action in a B-17 over Germany in March 1944. Thinking about how devastating this kind of news would be for my parents was gut-wrenching.

Postville, Iowa, is a small town with a population of 960. I knew just about everyone, and they knew me. I once flew a B-17 at very low altitude down Main Street in Postville. It scared the hell out of many of the residents and woke up every baby in town. Articles about me appeared in the *Postville Herald*, the hometown newspaper. They wrote about my Air Corps career, including being the first B-29 pilot to bomb the Japanese homeland island and setting a speed record flying from the United States to India.

I drifted off to sleep, awakened only a few minutes later by Saltzman's moans.

"Saltzman, are you alright?" I asked.

"Do you have any more morphine?" he asked. "My hands feel like they are on fire, and my ankles are not much better."

"I hate to say it, Saltz, but what little morphine we had left I gave to Lindley earlier. I wish I could do something for you, but I don't know what else I can do right now."

Hansman looked at Saltzman and Lindley and said, "Maybe George and Georgette can lead us to a doctor. These two are in agony."

We were still lounging under the rubber trees when an older

Chinese man and a very slender boy around 12 years old came up the trail into the clearing and walked toward our group. The man was carrying a large pot of tea. George walked over from where he was resting to greet them. They chatted for a minute. Then George sent the boy back down the trail to act as a lookout for Jap patrols. George and the older Chinese man with his pot of tea joined Georgette, Saltzman, Lindley, Hansman, Duffy, and me. We were all having a splendid time just sitting around on the ground at the edge of the clearing, relaxing and enjoying some excellent mint-tasting tea.

As I took a drink of my tea, George sent his cup flying in the air and sprang to his feet. He stared in the direction of the trail like he heard something. It was a whistling signal from the young boy on the lookout for Japs on the trail. George looked nervous and motioned for us to stand. Duffy and I jumped up to see if we could see anyone coming up the trail. We did not see anybody. But then, while we helped Lindley and Saltzman to their feet, three Japanese soldiers wearing visor caps, brown uniforms, and leggings came running around the bend about 30 yards away.

Hansman yelled, "Japs!" and fell to his knees.

Their leader looked our way and, after spotting us, screamed something over his shoulder to the two other soldiers behind him. The three startled Japs came upon us so fast that they leaped back off the trail and tumbled into the underbrush to take cover.

Everybody at our tea party scattered in all directions. Before I could finish yelling "Go! Go! Go!" George had already taken off like a gazelle, and Georgette was right on his heels, leaving her bundle of clothing behind. They both ran into a nearby jungle thicket while I yanked Hansman back to his feet. Then I saw Duffy race by, close behind George and Georgette. When Hansman was on his feet again, he took a glance around and then followed right behind Duffy. I ran in a low crouch behind Hansman, expecting any moment to receive a bullet between my shoulder blades before I could reach the safety of the thicket and join the others.

Looking back as I entered the thicket, I was horrified to see Lindley

51

and Saltzman running in the opposite direction, straight at the Japs who were now coming back up the trail.

Lindley became confused and did not know why we all ran. When he saw the Japs, he leaped off the edge of the clearing into the brush. He jumped right into the hands of the enemy.

Saltzman was standing beside Lindley when I yelled "Go! Go! Go!" He also ran in the wrong direction, following close behind Lindley. But when he saw the Japs coming up the trail in front of Lindley, he put on the brakes and reversed his course. He could see the rest of us disappearing into the brush, so he headed in our direction as fast as his sore ankles could take him. He was halfway back across the clearing when a wide-eyed, very young-looking Japanese soldier came running into the cleared area from the other side with his rifle in hand. When the young soldier met Saltzman eye-to-eye 40 feet away, he stopped dead in his tracks. Maybe because of fear, he did not shoot. The young soldier jumped back to the clearing edge and yelled for the other soldiers. This momentary hesitation allowed Saltzman time to put his head down and jackrabbit in our direction. He dove into a nearby thicket out of sight. The Japanese patrol never fired a shot.

We all ran as fast and as best as we could in the thick brush. I could see George getting away from us as we left the rubber plantation's overgrown bush and plowed our way through the dense jungle. There were not any trails to follow, so the vines and branches slashed at our faces and ankles and snagged and ripped our clothes. I tripped over a hidden log and crashed to the ground. Duffy, trying to plow through some thick brush, threw his body like a linebacker at an entanglement of vines that bounced him back into a collision with Hansman. We needed to exert every ounce of energy we possessed to make any headway. Sometimes we had to back off, change direction, and try again to make any progress.

I felt as though I was spinning my wheels, but I knew that next to being shot or captured by the Japs, our most significant concern was losing George. He was our ticket out of this jungle to safety.

We kept pushing through the best we could. As the jungle thinned out a bit, I could see glimpses of George's green shirt through the brush ahead of us. His close-cropped hair bobbed up and down as he got farther away. Putting on a burst of speed with my long legs, I gained on George, grabbed his shoulder, and pulled him down to stop him.

The others, except for Lindley, caught up. I said as I gasped for breath, "Sit down and catch your breath. Let's rest a minute. George, I know you can't understand me, but this is what I am going to do if you try to leave us here in the middle of nowhere."

I pulled out my .45 and waved it in front of George's face. George got the message.

Hansman looked around and asked, "Where's Lindley? Has anyone seen him? Did the Japs get him?"

Duffy interrupted. "I didn't see where he went. Maybe we should go back to look for him."

Saltzman jumped in, saying, "I was running right behind him. I saw him run right into the Japs. They most likely grabbed him. I did not hear any shots, so they must have taken him alive. He was in no shape to run too far through this jungle anyway."

Duffy barked back, "I say we go back to find him. We cannot just leave him. We are not sure the Japs have him. Even if they do, we have guns."

I intervened. "I agree with Saltzman. I saw him as he was heading right for the Japs. It is a sure bet they captured him. I do not think we would accomplish much by shooting it out with these Japs. Besides, it may be the best thing that could happen to Lindley. I don't think he could have survived much longer in the jungle without treatment for his burns. The Japs are in a better position to give him the treatment he needs. I know it is tough to leave him behind, but I think he is where he has the best chance for survival. Now, we have to think about how to save ourselves from these Japs."

The men agreed this was the best course of action. We sat down, trying to turn our thoughts to our present predicament. We hadn't heard any more from the Jap patrol, but we also did not know where

53

they went. They could still be somewhere nearby. We proceeded with caution at a slower pace.

Hansman thought out loud, "The Japs could be waiting for reinforcements to seal off the area and surround us."

Saltzman replied, "It won't be long before the Japs tighten the noose."

A lot of different thoughts were going through our minds.

Duffy said, "This jungle is almost impossible to get through. Maybe we ought to find a suitable spot to hole up for a while. The Japs may figure we are miles away from here."

Saltzman added, "I'm for that. I'm so pooped I don't think I can go much farther through this crap."

With George and Georgette leading the way, we winded our way through a series of dense thickets until George signaled us to stop. Pointing ahead with his other hand cupped behind his ear, he listened. When he thought he heard something ahead of us, he became agitated and began motioning for us to be quiet.

Listening again, George showed us he could hear the faint sounds of a patrol through the silent jungle. Then we also heard Japanese voices far in the distance, and they were moving closer to our location. As the Japs came nearer and nearer, the six of us stood closer together. The Japs then encircled us, closing in from all directions. It was a pincer movement. The Japs were now everywhere.

We glanced at each other with bewildered expressions on our faces.

Turning to George, I placed my arms down at my sides and opened my palms, asking silently, "What do we do now, George? The Japs are closing in on us."

He motioned for us to follow him.

I looked at Duffy and whispered, "Duff, I guess we're taking your suggestion. It looks like George is finding us a place to hide."

A few minutes later, George pointed to an area surrounded by a thick clump of jungle brush and fallen trees. In Chinese and motioning with his hands, he told us this was as good a place as any to hole up.

With fallen leaves and the deep rotting vegetation covering the ground, it looked to me like this dense underbrush would provide us with sufficient concealment.

It was 10:00 on the morning of January 12th, day two since the crash. We burrowed into the ground cover and buried ourselves in the rotting leaves. While arranging the ground vegetation to create our concealed hideout beds, we discovered the ground cover was alive with crawling beetles, insects, and worms of all sizes and descriptions. The insects were delighted to see their new guests as they crawled inside our clothing and feasted to their hearts' content. It was torturous, but we remained as still as possible and tried to ignore them since we had no other option.

As Saltzman settled in, trying to hide under a blanket of leaves, he cried out, "Damn!" He sat up, clawing at his right ear, and screamed, "A bug crawled into my ear!"

Duffy growled back in a low voice, "Get the damn bug out of your ear and quiet down or the Japs are going to be all over us!"

It was not long after George found our hideout that we heard Jap patrols all around us. As their search grew nearer and nearer, the chattering, yelling, and bush beating intensified. Our hearts were in our mouths when the first patrol reached us and came within a few yards of our hideout. If anyone moved, we were dead ducks.

All of us had our pistols ready, and George held a grenade in his hand. Another Jap patrol headed in our direction and came close, but they went right on by us. We continued to lie quiet and still while the Japanese patrols searched the surrounding area. We could hear the bashing and thrashing of the Japanese machetes right next to us, but by the grace of God, we went undetected in our well-hidden burrows. A few minutes later, the sounds of patrol activity decreased as the Japs shifted away from our location, and then it seemed like all the Japs had left the area. We could now relax. We all took a deep sigh of relief. The only sounds we heard now were the usual jungle noises.

It was late morning and still quiet. I whispered to Hansman, "It's been a while since we heard the Japs leave this area. Maybe they have given up."

Hansman nodded. "Let's hope so. This damn waiting is driving me crazy. Besides, we have to get some medical attention for Saltzman."

Then we heard barking, and Saltzman yelled, "Dogs! The damn Japs are coming back with dogs!"

George leaped to his feet, chattering in Chinese to Georgette as he pointed toward the yapping dogs. We knew from George's actions that he feared the dogs would pick up our trail and lead the Japanese troops right to us. He grew more agitated as the sound of Japanese voices and dog yelps grew closer. He seemed undecided about what to do next. Should we leave or remain hidden and hope for the best? He and Georgette continued their animated discussion while the four of us grew more anxious. The Japs and their dogs were not far away. We needed to decide.

Duffy whispered to me, "That's where they went, Hump. They went to get the damn dogs."

I nodded and said, "Give me a minute to think, Duff."

Observing the pair's reaction to this recent development, I knew George and Georgette understood death was a certainty for them if they were captured. The Japs would execute them. I did not know if that same fate awaited my crew. However, it was common knowledge among American Airmen that the Japanese hated B-29 flyers because of the many civilian casualties caused by B-29 raids on the Japanese home islands. During the briefings, I saw documented evidence of the torture and execution of captured B-29 crews. But what also concerned me were the reports confirming the on-the-spot beheadings of captured U.S. Airmen.

After George and Georgette stopped talking, we decided it was better to stay in our hideout burrows. George and Georgette burrowed under the leaves and branches with us. Then we all held our breaths and waited.

Just minutes later, a single drum started beating in the distance, and the dogs stopped barking. We heard the Japanese voices drift away toward the drumbeat. Then once again, it was quiet. Perhaps the drum signal called off the patrol or sent the patrol to search in another direction.

It was now 2:00 in the afternoon, January 12th, and we had been hiding in this thicket since morning with little movement. George signaled for everyone to continue to lie low.

I whispered to Duffy, "That was a close one."

Duffy whispered back, "I don't think we are out of this mess yet. They might bring those damn dogs back this way."

Half an hour later, George crawled out of our hiding place. He listened in all directions and studied the nearby jungle. He seemed concerned about the Japs leaving someone in the area as a lookout. Motioning for us to stay put, he went to scout around.

An hour later, George reappeared in a more relaxed mood. He and Georgette exchanged a few words, and in sign language, George told us the Japanese troops had left the area, and there were Chinese all around who would warn us if any Japs returned.

I realized George and Georgette were part of an organization of people working together deep within this vast jungle to resist the Japanese invaders they had grown to despise. It was now clear they had prearranged the time and place of the previous meeting for the Malay native Talib to hand us off to this pair of Chinese guides. From the start, under someone's instruction, Talib's job was to bring us to meet George and Georgette. It seemed to be a kind of jungle underground. That George could talk to the Chinese during his short time away seemed to support this.

Once again, using his unique sign language, which we were now beginning to understand, George showed us we could move around, but we would need to remain here for a while.

As we rose to our feet and brushed off the insects and leaves from our flight suits, I pondered the loss of Lindley. It weighed on my conscience to make such a decision, but in my heart, I knew it was the right one. I also wondered about the fate of the other six—Billings, Govednik, Kundrat, MacDonald, Gillett, and Spratt. Were they alive or dead? I hoped they survived the crash and joined up with the

Australian and British soldiers Talib mentioned and weren't captured by the Japanese.

At mid-afternoon, we started again. Trudging through the animal trails became a test of endurance. We were out of our element. Our Chinese guides appeared tireless. Walking for hours barefoot did not bother them, but our feet became blistered and cut by the rough elephant trails and the thick brush. It was an extra formidable challenge for Saltzman because of his burnt lower legs, but with a trance-like motion, he continued to hobble along, pushing himself forward.

Darkness set in on the second day as the four of us plodded along behind George and Georgette, one behind the other. We had not eaten since early the previous morning, and hunger further sapped our strength. About midnight, too exhausted to proceed any farther, Saltzman grabbed my arm and said weakly, "I can't go on, Hump. I have had it. Can we please take a break?"

Just as I was ready to stop George to give Saltzman a rest, I noticed the jungle had thinned out and George had slowed down. George stopped just ahead of me and placed his index finger on his lips, telling us to be quiet. He then started forward and pointed toward the clearing ahead.

Peering through the darkness with a bit of moonlight to help, I could make out a concrete highway running alongside some railroad tracks about 100 yards ahead. Beside the railroad tracks was a small farmhouse. George spoke with Georgette for a few minutes, and then Georgette gestured for us to sit on the ground. We were more than happy to comply with her request. It was now hard to stay standing.

Georgette joined us and sat on the ground while George walked toward the farmhouse. We watched as a Chinese man wearing a white shirt came out of the house and headed for the latrine behind the house. George slipped up to the farmhouse side and waited for the Chinese man to come out. The farmer appeared startled to see George. After a few words, the man ran into the house and slammed the door behind him. Whatever it was George said, it scared the man back into the safety of his home. George signaled for us to follow him as he headed for the nearby railroad tracks.

With some groans and moans, we all struggled to our feet. We were hungry, thirsty, and exhausted from the equatorial heat that drained our fluids. The jungle trees and brush had cut us from head to toe. And along with the never-ending, blood-sucking mosquito attacks, all kinds of insect and worm bites covered our bodies. Saltzman still suffered from his burns, and Duffy struggled with finger and side injuries.

While limping and hobbling, we pushed forward the best we could to follow Georgette to the tracks and keep pace with the ever-moving and tireless George.

As we crossed the railroad tracks, Saltzman pointed down the tracks to our right. "Listen! Can you guys hear a train coming?"

I stopped to look down the tracks. Through the trees, I could make out the flicker of a headlamp coming around the bend 150 yards away.

"Get off the tracks!" I shouted as I jumped down between the railroad tracks and the road into a shallow, brush-filled ditch. The others tumbled in behind me just as the headlamp of the speeding train lit up the railroad tracks above us. Pressing our bodies into the ground, we stared up at the railcars thundering by only a few feet away. All the windows of the train cars were wide open with the interior lights on. It was a troop train overflowing with Japanese soldiers and heading north. Windblown Nips without helmets hung their heads out the windows and stared into the darkness of the night, right into our eyes.

As the last car passed, Duffy exclaimed, "Damn, that was close! Let's get the hell out of here before anything else comes along."

As we rose to our feet to climb back up the bank to cross the road, truck lights appeared on the highway coming from the south and illuminated the entire area. We jumped back off the road and ducked down into the ditch again. When the truck drew near, we could see bayonets in the back of the vehicle glistening in the moonlight. I knew the ditch offered minimal concealment in the bright lights, but we hid in the deep weeds the best we could. Unlike the massive, fast-moving train, I knew the truck could stop right in front of us if they saw us hiding in the ditch.

I whispered, "Draw your .45s now, and be ready in case we're spotted."

Perhaps with some help from the Man above, we went unnoticed as the truck filled with Japanese troops cruised on by us less than 10 feet away. I crawled toward George when I noticed him pointing at a man on the road ahead of the truck. I could see a uniformed Chinese Quisling standing guard for the Japanese about 30 yards away in the headlight beams. He appeared relaxed as he stood in the middle of the road puffing on a cigarette with a rifle in his hand. The Chinese stared at the truck coming toward him and then moved off to the side of the roadway to allow it to pass. He seemed to be unaware of our existence nearby, maybe because of the brightness of the lights in his eyes.

Saltzman said under his breath, "Hump, I think the Japs placed this guy here to spot us when we crossed the road. What are we going to do now?"

As I was thinking things over, I glanced over at George. He motioned for us to be quiet and not move. Then George crawled about 15 yards up the ditch, and when he was behind the sentry, he said something to him in Chinese. Startled, the guard dropped his cigarette and spun around, ready to shoot. George said something else in Chinese. The sentry hesitated for a few seconds as if thinking it over and then lowered his gun. George then signaled for us to come on up to join him as the guard turned his back and allowed us to cross. We slipped across the road in single file while keeping our eyes on the guard. Then we back-stepped into the jungle on the other side. I touched George's arm and pointed back in the direction of the guard. George, breaking into a rare grin, said in pidgin English, "I say, 'You make trouble, you be dead!'" Those were the first and last English words I ever heard out of George.

At sunrise on day three, January 13, 1945, our two Chinese friends guided us out of the dense jungle. We hiked along some animal trails that ran through several abandoned farms. As the day went on, George grew angry at us because of our slow pace. Even though we did our best to stay with him, he often turned around to admonish us in

Chinese to speed up. But nothing George could say or do motivated us to move any faster. We had not slept. We had not eaten. And over the past 48 hours, we had experienced the most excruciating physical and mental ordeals of our lives. We were now walking on willpower alone.

CHAPTER 5

Commander Hog

B ecause of a never-ending trek looming ahead, the temptation
grew to order George to stop for a rest. However, we placed
our trust in these two Chinese, and so far, it was working out.
You might even call it miraculous. Because of their familiarity with the
area and jungle life, the four of us had eluded the Japanese Army. With
the single exception of losing Lindley, George and Georgette had
proved to be a godsend. I felt sure the Japanese troops would have
rounded us up by now without our two Chinese guides' help.

The Japanese grabbing Lindley was the best thing that could
happen to him. He needed urgent treatment for his burns, and maybe

he would get it from his captors. He would not have received the treatment he needed to survive if he were here with us in the jungle. Still, his fate weighed on my mind.

I decided not to interfere with George as he seemed to know what he was doing. If George felt it was necessary to keep going to avoid the Japs, so be it. We would have to persevere and keep moving.

We did our best to keep up with George's fast pace. That afternoon, as we crossed through a large clearing, we saw three Chinese emerging out of the jungle on the far side. As we approached, they walked out of the bush to meet us. It stunned us when the newcomers berated George and Georgette in rapid-fire Chinese. The three waiting Chinese were upset because we were late for this rendezvous.

Duffy whispered to me, "Now we know why George kept pushing us so hard. It looks like he was trying to keep on a schedule, and we were running late."

"Yeah," I replied. "I wonder how they knew we were coming. There must be an underground jungle grapevine."

It seemed the Chinese had an organized and fast communication system with runners stationed from place to place.

Addressing the Chinese men, I asked, "Do you speak English?"

With no response, I turned to Duffy. "I wish we could talk to these guys to get an idea of where they're taking us. Talib spoke about Australians and British being around here somewhere. Maybe they will take us to the Allies' camp where there will be a radio we can use."

After settling the lateness matter, the group of five Chinese turned and headed back into the bush. George motioned for us to follow. After climbing a steep, tree-covered hill, we arrived at a basha in a narrow clearing.

The basha appeared to be a typical Malayan jungle house. It resembled a small bungalow with window blinds made of bamboo slats covering the two front windows. It was around 15 feet by 15 feet square with a thatched roof that extended over a rickety veranda constructed of logs. The entire structure was 3 feet off the ground on posts away from the insects and animals.

As soon as we entered, we dropped to the bamboo floor in the almost empty one-room house. Its remote location, along with its non-family environment, seemed to show it was a meeting place—a hideout post—for these Chinese.

A pot containing a duck was boiling on a small fire in the center of the room. One of the Chinese, a colossal coolie who would have been a shoo-in to play left tackle for the Chicago Bears, motioned for us to help ourselves.

Hansman looked in the boiling pot and whispered, "Look! They have the whole damn duck in there! Head, bill, feet, guts, everything."

I said, "Dig in, gang. It looks like it's our introduction to Chinese cooking."

While I sat on the floor eating boiled duck with my fingers, I looked over at our Chinese companions. One of them was a well-groomed young man in his 20s who wore white shorts and a button-down shirt. He could have passed for an Ivy League college student. But the resemblance ended right there. When he picked up his bowl to eat, he thrust his face and hands deep into the bowl and shoveled the duck into his mouth as fast as he could. He devoured his food so quickly that I was surprised he could swallow it without choking. Because he was the first of the Chinese to help himself to the pot after we took our portions, I assumed he was the leader of this little group. And because he ate so fast, we nicknamed him Commander Hog.

The third man had a crippled right arm and was dressed in ragged clothes. He was short, thin, and filthy, and always seemed to have a small grin on his face. We later learned a Japanese bullet had damaged his arm during an earlier battle.

As soon as we arrived, Georgette took Saltzman by the arm and led him to the corner of the basha. She was a beautiful Chinese girl, and by the gleam in her eye, you could see she thought Saltzman was a handsome specimen. First, Georgette filled a bowl of food for Saltzman and fed him. When he finished eating, Georgette took a pan of boiling water from the open fire to bathe his burned hands. She cleaned them, and then with a comforting smile, she pulled off the dead, blackened skin piece by little piece. Then she washed the backs of his hands clean. When she finished, you could see the white bones and tendons against the raw red flesh on the back of Saltzman's hands from his knuckles up to his wrists. She repeated the same warmhearted tender care for his ankles and ears.

When she finished, she went over and sat beside Commander Hog. Their conversation lasted for quite a while, with both looking back at Saltzman. We could not understand what they said since it was in Chinese, but we could tell it concerned Saltzman. When they finished their conversation, Commander Hog called the grinning Chinese over, talked with him a minute, and sent him out of the basha.

Sometime later, a Chinese came running out of the jungle over to the basha and handed Commander Hog a small bottle. Commander Hog called Georgette over to his side. They chatted for a minute, and he gave her the bottle. She looked pleased when she accepted the bottle and went right back to Saltzman, took him by the arm, and started covering his burns with the contents of the handmade container. Georgette smiled during this entire process while Saltzman groaned and moaned with pain. He was in a great deal of pain but with patience endured the treatment by pretty Georgette. When Georgette finished, she gave Saltzman another big smile and left.

After we finished eating and the Chinese kept guard outside the basha, there was some time to relax and sleep. After a few hours of sleep and just before dark, we moved out again with Commander Hog leading the way. The third night's trek was terrible. Saltzman was nearing delirium and always needed our full attention to keep him from wandering away. The terrain became rougher and rougher through thick jungle with its narrow paths and many hills to climb, but we pushed forward without knowing where we were going.

Several hours later when we emerged from the thick jungle, we were relieved to see a small clearing. Two bashas that looked almost the same as the one we just left were on one side. As Commander Hog led us forward, we could not see any light coming from either basha. The area looked deserted. It was quiet except for the rustle of some small animals somewhere in the brush.

From out of the darkness, somewhere in front of us, we heard a loud voice speaking to us in perfect English. "Good evening, Americans. You are safe from the Japanese Army here. You are now in the Second Regiment outpost of the Communist Anti-Jap Army of Malaya."

It surprised me to hear this voice speaking to us in English. I searched to find the speaker's face in the dim light of the full moon. It was a young Chinese man about 17 or 18 years old. He grinned a knowing grin as he watched me stare at him. The young man motioned for us to come inside one of the bashas. He said he would show us where we could sleep. Sleep! That was music to our ears.

We entered a room lit by a small oil lamp and saw our sleeping quarters for the night, a 20-foot wide bed constructed of many stakes driven into the ground with saplings stretched across them. Large palm leaves spread on top of the bamboo saplings created a flat surface where we could sleep two feet above the ground. We had some company. Thousands of insects were crawling and nesting all over the sapling bed, and eight dirty Chinese were already on the bed sleeping. The young man jumped up next to the Chinese, and with a stick, he prodded the eight Chinese to move over and make room for the four of us to lie down. He then said, "Goodnight, Americans," and left. Crawling bugs and eight dirty Chinese men did not matter to us because we were more dingy and offensive smelling than they were, and we were exhausted. So Hansman, Duffy, Saltzman, and I tumbled into bed and passed out.

The next morning, day four in the jungle, the Chinese English-speaking young man came in early and nudged me to wake me up. He asked, "Are you the commanding officer?"

I nodded and said, yes. He then told me the commanding officer of this Communist Anti-Jap Army outpost wanted to see me. On the way to the commander's basha, I asked the young man how he spoke English so well. The young man said he received his education in an American missionary school near Singapore. He told me his Chinese name was Foo-Lee Wong, but the missionaries had christened him Bartholomew.

When I entered the commander's basha with Bartholomew, there was Commander Hog, the impatient and angry Chinese who had met us in the jungle with George and Georgette the day before. He was also the dapper young man who stuffed himself with the duck at our evening meal, which is how he earned our nickname Commander Hog. He was also the same Commander Hog who led us to this camp the night before.

It turned out that Commander Hog was the Communist commanding officer of this outpost. He opened our conversation with a typical formal Chinese-style introduction. Hog bowed and told Bartholomew to tell me how glad he was we had escaped and that he would keep us safe from the Japanese. I thanked him and told him how grateful we were to him for his help. We then got down to the meat of why Commander Hog wanted to meet with me. As he talked, our conversation turned into his bitter tirade against the white man, but mainly against the British.

Hog said when the British fled Malaya because of the Japanese invasion from the north, the British officers told him they would soon be back to help the Chinese fight the Japanese. Then he said, with bitterness in his voice, that after they left, no British troops ever came back to help. Because of their lack of support, the Japanese killed or tortured thousands of people in Malaya.

Then Hog proclaimed that his Communist Anti-Jap Army with thousands of men was ready to fight the Japanese. They just lacked the adequate arms and equipment to fight. His native Army was fighting the Japanese Army with a small collection of weapons found abandoned by the British Army during their flight south through the Malay Peninsula when Japan invaded in 1942.

Hog said the Chinese Communist leaders of Malaya pleaded with the British officers to give them all their weapons before they surrendered to the Japanese, but they refused. Instead, they cached all the guns and equipment in the jungle in secret hiding places all over

Malaya just before their surrender. The Chinese guerrillas searched for them but could only find a few of the cached weapons. Hog went on for more than an hour incriminating the British and taking a few cracks at the United States that also had not come to their rescue.

Bartholomew's promise that there wouldn't be any Japanese in this area turned out to be short-lived. One of the outside sentries came running into the camp yelling, "Nippon Li! Nippon Li!"

Everyone jumped up, grabbed their meager belongings, and followed Commander Hog out of the camp into the jungle. It was 4:30 in the afternoon, and with the area overrun with the Japanese, we were on the run again.

Hog was in the lead, followed by another Chinese guerrilla, George, Georgette, Bartholomew, Hansman, Duffy, Saltzman, me, and three more Chinese with rifles. We were on the move away from the Japs.

We followed another jungle trail marked with a lot of fresh animal tracks. This area must have been the home of many elephants because elephant tracks and elephant dung were everywhere. We could see dried mud where elephants scraped against the tree trunks along the trail. The mud was several feet above our heads, showing the size of the enormous Asian elephants. We could not identify many other animal tracks except for one that looked like the imprint of a sizable cat's paw, maybe a tiger or leopard.

Hog and the Chinese guerrilla led the way and carried large machetes to slash through the vines and undergrowth. As they chopped their way forward, I heard loud yelps twice when they cut the heads off two giant green snakes. Bartholomew said the green snakes always hid at the edge of the trail, hoping to snatch a meal coming by.

We followed Commander Hog for about 20 minutes at a pace as fast as the jungle would allow. Then he turned off the animal trail and led us into what looked like a green jungle wall. Hog and the other Chinese guide tried to hack and slash their way through it with their machetes for several minutes, and then they stopped. It was too thick. Hog ordered everyone to sit down in an undergrowth area so dense you could only see a few feet around. I felt like the Japanese would never find us in this. Hog motioned for everyone to sit and be quiet. We hid and waited.

After a few minutes, I heard some rustling in the trees above. I looked up to see 20 or 30 monkeys studying us. As I sat observing them, I was considering what they thought of their unknown visitors. I wondered if their impression of us was favorable after they studied us for a while. After about an hour, the monkeys relaxed and talked among themselves.

A runner came and said something in Chinese to Hog. Then Hog told Bartholomew to tell us the Japs left the area and we could now go back to the camp. We followed him back to camp, slipping and sliding on the muddy path to the animal trail, and soon made it back to the basha. We rested in Commander Hog's Second Regiment Anti-Jap Army outpost until January 15th.

On day five, January 15th, Commander Hog informed us that they needed to take us to a new, safer location farther into the bush. That night we left with our new group now composed of our new guide Nippon Joe, four bodyguards, George, Georgette, Bartholomew, Hansman, Saltzman, Duffy, and me. Hog stayed back as the commander of the Second Regiment outpost. During the next three treacherous nights, we would agonize at each turn as we traveled through the black dripping wet jungle. This trip introduced us to jungle swamplands with water up to our chests.

Saltzman got into trouble right off the bat. We had just started into the bush from the outpost when he became disoriented and walked off the trail again. He fell and went down another steep bank 20 feet deep. Almost all the bits of skin left on his burned hands ripped away on this fall, adding to his misery. As if he wasn't suffering enough from his body covered in burn wounds, he now also had a scraped-up face. The burns surrounding his eyes caught up to him, and he could no longer see where he was going. The bodyguards had to hold him up so the group could stay on the move. They sometimes stopped to give him drinks of water to keep him hydrated, but he was out of it. The rest of this trip was a foggy delirium for him.

On January 16th, the second day of this new journey and the sixth day of walking into the depths of the Malayan jungle, we waded through a swamp with water sometimes up to our necks and leeches everywhere. The first thing I noticed was Georgette tearing at her legs and crying while the Chinese guerrillas laughed at her. These Chinese were no gentlemen to the rescue. In their minds, everybody was on their own.

Then I felt like something was dripping down my right leg. When I jerked up my pant leg, I saw a big unsightly round hole in my calf with blood pouring out. On my shoe top was a two-inch brown blob crawling toward my heel. It was a jungle leech gorged with my blood.

They were among the principal curses of jungle life. Their bite became infected and turned into something like a huge boil. Just when you thought it was healing, it would break open again with dripping pus. Scars from the ulcers were typical after they healed. It was common to see Chinese with large round leech bite ulcers six inches across. They sometimes treated them by putting tobacco ashes into the wound, or they would seek the services of an "outside doctor."

When we reached the other side of the swamp, we sat down to take turns pulling leeches off each other. The leeches emitted an antiseptic of some sort before putting their heads under your skin to fill themselves with your blood, so it wasn't likely that you felt them when they were in the act. They could be all over you, feasting on your blood, and you would not feel a thing. They covered our entire bodies—on our legs, in our ears, in our hair, all over us.

When Bartholomew saw us pulling the leeches off, he ran over and told us to stop. He went back over to Nippon Joe and returned with a lighted cigarette. Bartholomew started touching each of the blood-sucking little monsters with the fiery end of the lit cigarette, and they dropped off. He explained that when we pulled these blood-sucking parasites off, we were leaving their heads under our skin, which would cause them to become infected. Later, the infections could turn into jungle ulcers. If the leeches became full of your blood, they would withdraw their heads and fall off. The hole would heal, with the only damage being the loss of your blood.

Bartholomew explained that if we did not smoke, we could also touch the leeches with raw tobacco or salt, and they would drop off. But it was too late. We had already pulled several of these slimy bloodsuckers off, leaving their heads under our skin. All of us ended up with jungle ulcers sometime later. I had saved one small two-inch paper packet of sulfa powder from my parachute jungle kit, so we debated whether to use it on the leech bites or save it. With Saltzman still in terrible condition with severe burns, we kept the sulfa powder for later.

When Duffy unbuttoned his shirt to check for leeches, he exposed his black and blue, bruised chest. It looked serious.

I asked Duffy, "Are you passing blood?"

"First two days I did, but it quit. I'm sure it's the ribs, Hump," Duff answered.

"How about breathing?" I asked. "Talking seems to put a strain on you. Do you think you punctured a lung?"

"There's a pain when I breathe, but it's the up and down movement of my rib cage. I don't think it's a lung," he replied.

Duffy said he could continue. So after we finished tending to all the leech bites from our swamp adventure, we started back on our journey. After walking a while, a Chinese man appeared from a jungle trail to join us. Bartholomew said he was an outside doctor who wanted to walk with us through the jungle to the next guerrilla camp. He would treat two high-ranking Communist Anti-Jap Army officers stationed there. The outside doctor walked with us all day until we arrived at the next camp deep in the jungle.

Bartholomew took us to the main palm-roofed basha to meet the Communist Army big wheel. He could not speak any English but conversed in Chinese with Bartholomew, who acted as an interpreter for us. The Chinese Army officer showed us a colossal jungle ulcer on his right leg, just above his knee. It was a seeping ulcer that started with a leech bite. They explained that with the high moisture and heat in the jungle, the infection would grow bigger and bigger if not treated by an outside doctor. If the doctor could not give him something that would heal the humongous ulcer, it would kill the man.

The outside doctor walked over to the Communist Army officer and examined the jungle ulcer. They rattled back and forth in Chinese for several minutes, and then the outside doctor turned and left the basha.

When the doctor left, another Chinese led us to a small basha in the camp and said we could rest there for the night. After checking the basha, we went down to a nearby stream because our cut and bitten bodies needed a bath. After being refreshed by the semi-cool water in the stream, Bartholomew surprised us with some rice and cooked greens that looked like spinach leaves the camp cook had gathered in the jungle. I thought, "Better than no Spam," and we sat down to eat.

Most of the time, we went to sleep when it turned dark, but tonight was different. Bartholomew called us over to the Chinese officer's basha just as the outside doctor returned. The doctor did not look like a doctor. He was short, perhaps 35 years old, and very skinny. He had no shoes, shirt, or trousers but only a loincloth with rattan tied around his waist as a belt. The doctor was not an M.D. but a Chinese herb doctor.

The only light was from a half coconut shell filled with coconut oil with a small wick. In the dim lamplight, the outside doctor held up what Bartholomew said was a monitor lizard. The brown monitor lizard was huge, about 15 feet long. Bartholomew said they liked to eat small animals and lived near the water. They could move fast, were dangerous, and had killed men. The outside doctor held it by one short front leg. Its head was a foot long, and out of its mouth hung a red, 10- to 12-inch split tongue dripping with blood. The dim light from the coconut shell made the whole scene seem like something out of the Dark Ages. After examining his lizard, the herb doctor looked up at us with a smile and said something in Chinese. Bartholomew interpreted. "He says, 'Good for jungle ulcer.'"

We watched as the doctor cut open the skull of the monitor lizard.

After he scooped out the part of the brain he needed, he dropped it into a tin cup. Then he cut up and washed some roots or herbs he had stored in a small bag tied to his rattan belt. He dropped them into the tin cup, added water to the mixture, and put it over the fire to boil.

After cooking the cup's contents for a short time, he took the tin cup off the fire and set it aside to cool. A few moments later, the outside doctor removed a leaf from his rattan belt, dipped it into the cooled broth, and used the wet leaf blade to clean the Communist officer's jungle ulcer. He washed the ulcer for several minutes, going up and down and around the ulcer several times, sometimes dipping the leaf back into his mixture. Satisfied with his work, he took several odd-shaped leaves from his belt and laid them side by side over the jungle ulcer. He poured the remaining broth from the cup over the leaves that covered the ulcer.

During the treatment, the stoic Chinese Communist Anti-Jap Army officer sat without moving and never uttered a sound. Bartholomew said the remedy was excruciating but would cure the ulcer. I asked Bartholomew why he called him an outside doctor. He explained that if you have something wrong with you inside, you need an inside doctor. If you have something wrong with you on the outside of your body, you need an outside doctor. Medical specialists, even in the Malayan jungle.

We could not stay around to see the treatment results because the Chinese guerrilla, Nippon Joe, told us to rest up because we would leave the next day.

The following day and for the next day and a half, we traveled through some less dense but still thick jungle. About noon on January 18th, the eighth day since the *Postville Express* crashed, we arrived at another small Communist Anti-Jap Army outpost. Only around 25 soldiers garrisoned this camp with 10 bashas and one larger hut. A huge curly-haired man came rushing out of the larger hut to meet us. He pumped our hands like a Hollywood press agent. That is why we called him Hollywood.

He spoke excellent English. Hollywood told us his mother was a

Jamaican Negro and his father a Chinese. They brought him from Jamaica to Malaya when he was a child. He seemed well educated, and it soon became apparent that he was a rabid Communist and hated the British. Back at the Second Regiment outpost, we heard Commander Hog's rantings about the British. Now Hollywood told us the complete story about British imperialism, the Japanese oppression in Malaya, and the Communist movement that developed because of these two evils.

Hollywood explained that the English always held both the Malays and the Chinese in Malaya under rigid restrictions. The British owned all the commerce and rubber plantations. If the Malays and hard-working Chinese remained as a coolie class and cheap labor, the British fortunes would grow, which was the purpose of all the restrictions. The British goal was to assimilate most of the country's wealth into British hands.

Hollywood said word had trickled through the grapevine into Malaya about a great and mighty nation concerned about the Malays and Chinese sufferings in Malaya and wanted to help. Then, with a proud look on his face, he told us the name of that nation—Soviet Russia.

The British had controlled the Malay Peninsula for more than 60 years. Despite the watchful nature of the British, the Russian Communist information pamphlets and Russian books filled with propaganda found their way into Malaya. This literature proclaimed how Russia won its freedom from slavery under similar conditions. They told how, in the land of the hammer and sickle, they assured even the humblest man or woman an adequate livelihood and education.

Hollywood explained how the former Chinese leaders formed a Communist Party in Malaya. One or two of these former leaders disappeared from Malaya for several years. When they returned, they were well-educated men who spoke fluent French and Russian, making them even better leaders.

Hollywood went on for hours about how Communism developed in Malaya. He told us the Communist Party began organizing in 1925 and gained ground in the country despite the frantic attempts by the British to stamp it out.

In the 1890s with the help of the British, immigrants came from Southern China and Southern India to work in the British tin mines and on British rubber plantations. The conditions became horrendous for these laborers. Most of the Communist Party recruits came from the ranks of these Chinese coolies who desired a better life free of British oppression and persecution.

Hollywood explained that the current Communist Anti-Jap Army, led by a mysterious, well-educated man, numbered in the thousands of Chinese guerrillas scattered throughout Malaya. As far back as the early 1930s, this man was one of the top Communists in the country. Hollywood told us he had never seen this mysterious leader, and he did not even know his name. The Communist Army Command granted only the highest officers of the Communist Anti-Jap Army admittance into the same room of this Supreme Commander of the Central Military Committee of the Communist Anti-Jap Army.

But Hollywood knew a little about the mysterious leader. He told us this man was reputed to be a native of French Indochina. Like many other party leaders before the war, he was in British jails several times on charges of Communist activity, but the British never realized the importance of the man they held captive and always let him go.

Hollywood said the British disposed of many prominent Malayan Communist leaders through an arrangement with Generalissimo Chiang Kai-shek of China. If the English caught one of these leaders, they deported him to China. According to Hollywood, when Chiang's men received a captured Chinese through this secret underground highway, that was the end of him. Because the English underestimated this leader's importance while he was in their jails, the Supreme Commander escaped this demise.

On December 8, 1941, right after midnight local Malaya time and just hours before attacking Pearl Harbor, the Japanese attacked the British Royal Air Force and the Australian Air Force base of operations in Northern Malaya at Kota Bharu. The Japanese drove the Allies south through the Malay Peninsula to Singapore. On February 15, 1942, the British surrendered to the Japanese in Singapore, giving Japan control of the critical and strategic Singapore Naval Base and the world's largest floating dry docks. It had been the mission of the *Postville Express* crew to bomb one of those Japanese-occupied Navy dry docks, the King George VI Graving Dock.

Hollywood said the Malay Peninsula was quiet the first year after the British surrendered to the Japanese in February 1942. During this time, the Chinese Communist guerrillas dispersed throughout the Malayan jungles to search for the cached weapons the British left behind during their escape from Northern Malaya to Singapore. They also began the widespread distribution of Communist propaganda that helped recruit fighting men for the growing Communist Party Army.

When the Japs arrived, Hollywood said, many of the Malay natives welcomed them because they thought it meant liberation from British oppression. The Japanese behaved well at first. They promised each man a patch of land and distributed the goods abandoned by the English when they retreated. They even gave away the automobiles the British left behind.

But over time, two things changed the people's minds in Malaya. One was the behavior of the Japanese Army. The Japanese became brutal once they felt they held the country under their rule. They began hunting and assassinating the Communist leaders and brutally executed thousands of Chinese and Malay people.

The Chinese Communist Party changed its name from the Communist Party of Malaya to the Malayan Peoples Anti-Jap Army. This name change helped recruit many Chinese who had grown to hate the Japanese. The other reason was the growing influence of the Communist propaganda circulating throughout Malaya. The Communists distributed this propaganda through the many Communist outposts established all over Malaya.

Again, Hollywood proudly told us he was Propaganda Chief for the Second Regiment. The Chinese Anti-Jap Army positioned secret radios deep in the jungle that picked up news broadcasts. Mimeograph machines turned out thousands of copies of newspapers and Russian propaganda pamphlets. The Communist Chinese then distributed the newspapers and propaganda literature to the Junior Propaganda Officers throughout the growing Communist Party organization.

The Chinese Propaganda Chiefs printed newspapers in Malay, Chinese, and English. The papers were known as *Voice of Liberty*, *The Victory Herald*, and *Voice of Malaya*. These newspapers gave the native people the only outside news available, and they also included editorials criticizing the British. The Chinese Communist sold Communism to the Malayan people under the disguise of anti-Jap rhetoric.

We were in Hollywood's camp for three days. At his suggestion, we wrote a letter to the Supreme Commander of the Communist Anti-Jap Army, explaining how we ended up in Malaya and asking for help to escape. A runner took our message and vanished deep into the jungle. While we waited for an answer, we just loafed. We felt safe from the Japanese Army at this camp located so deep in the wilderness. And by this time, we had become immune to the fear of them.

We tried to learn to eat with chopsticks, but the only food was a thin rice gruel. It was like eating oatmeal with two pencils. On the second day in camp, we found a native barber who lived nearby to cut our shaggy hair. Our newfound barber came equipped with six fingers on each hand and a hole cut on the side of each shoe for an extra toe that stuck out halfway back toward his instep. He was a darn good barber, too.

In the evenings, we sat in the basha listening to Hollywood while he delivered his passionate Chinese lectures to the guerrillas stationed at his Second Regiment outpost. We asked the English-speaking Bartholomew what Hollywood's topic was for this evening's speech. Bartholomew said he praised Russia and Communism and told his Chinese audience how they could build a new world right here in Malaya if they listened to the voice of the Soviets.

Here in Hollywood's camp, Saltzman met the young Chinese girl who saved his burned hands, if not his life. They were in terrible shape, filled with infection, and useless.

As we came into the camp, this girl we came to call Giggling Gertie for apparent reasons ran up to Saltzman after seeing his bandaged, burnt hands. Giggling Gertie inspected his burns, led him off to a nearby basha, and motioned him to sit down. Giggling the entire time, Giggling Gertie sat down beside Saltzman with a pair of old blood-stained brass tweezers and some boiling water and went to work on his hands. First, she washed off the burned spots, and then with the tweezers, she scraped or ripped off all the loose skin and blisters. When Saltzman flinched or cursed with pain, Giggling Gertie just giggled, smiled her pretty smile, and then went right back to ripping his skin off. When she finished cleaning the burns, she put a wet dressing on his hands. She kept repeating this same process again and again for the three days we were there.

Giggling Gertie had done the best she could, but Saltzman's hands were worsening. There was a very thick layer of seepage starting to develop an almost solid layer of crust that looked like hardened yellow pus. A red streak was moving up each of his arms, so I decided we should talk about this situation before the infection became a threat to his life.

I asked Saltzman what he wanted us to do. "Should we cut your hands off to stop the infection before it moves too far?"

Saltzman said his dad always told him, "Let nature take its course, and you will be alright."

I said, "Then we should use the one package of sulfa powder on the back of your hands to stop the infection."

"No!" Saltz shouted. "There is not enough sulfa to do my hands any good. Somebody else may need it later for something worse."

Everybody was there, and we decided Saltzman should have the final say. We left it there. He said, "Let nature take its course," and that is what we did.

CHAPTER 6

The Fever

On January 21st, the 11th day since we bailed out of the *Postville Express*, a letter arrived from the commanding officer of a higher-level headquarters directing us to his guerrilla garrison hidden even farther into the rainforest. After spending three days with Hollywood, we left that day with Nippon Joe, Bartholomew, and three Chinese guards armed with submachine guns and British-made rifles.

We parted company with George and Georgette who had helped us survive many close encounters with the Japanese. They would no longer be joining us on our journey as we moved deeper into the jungle to the next camp. Their responsibility for us was over. With Bartholomew translating, we thanked them for risking their lives to save ours. We told them we would never forget their acts of courageous kindness, and we bade them farewell.

After four hours and six miles of plodding through the dark, dense jungle, we reached the new Communist camp late in the afternoon. As we walked into the clearing, the outpost commander greeted us. He was a serious-looking, cold-eyed Chinese named Yung Han. The camp commander spoke some broken English, just enough to get his point across. He introduced us to a man named Lowe-Shin, one of his men from a nearby guerrilla outpost. This tall, slender Chinese who spoke almost perfect English was Yung Han's interpreter, and later, he would interpret for us. We named him English Tom. After being introduced to Lowe-Shin, I asked Yung Han, "Do you have a radio in this camp?"

Yung Han answered, "No radio here. Radio at Supreme Headquarters."

Then Yung Han said there would be a party in our honor later that evening and instructed Lowe-Shin—English Tom—to show us to our sleeping quarters. English Tom escorted us to one of the small bashas scattered around the camp.

Yung Han said the only radio was at Supreme Headquarters, and since there was no radio here, we realized this was not Supreme Headquarters. We settled in to rest awhile before the festivities began.

More established than the others, this camp had five large, rectangular bashas, each occupied by eight to 10 men, and other small bashas scattered here and there. That evening, they set up the largest basha in the camp for the party.

At around dusk, Yung Han came to our basha and escorted us to the festivities. There were around 40 men already gathered there when Yung Han walked in with us. Everyone jumped to their feet and, with clenched fists, saluted their commander. Yung Han showed us to our seats and went straight to the front of the basha hut to say a few Chinese words to his soldiers.

When Yung Han finished, everybody in the room, again with clenched fists held high, sang the "International" song. When they finished singing, everyone sat down, and five Chinese from the audience stepped up, one after the other, to make speeches. We knew they were talking about us because everybody kept looking in our direction during each spiel, and there was exuberant clapping and smiles all around after each spirit-filled oration. Bartholomew and English Tom were not there, so we had no way of knowing what the speakers were saying, but the soldiers all smiled and nodded in our direction during and after the speeches. We were lucky they knew we were American B-29 Airmen. The air support was the only part of the Allied war effort that ever helped the Malay people. These Chinese were showing us their gratitude.

After the speeches, two Chinese walked up to the front of the room to sing a Russian marching song, which sounded strange in Chinese. All the Chinese merrily pounded their feet—left, right, left, right—in cadence with the music. When the two Chinese finished their song, they motioned for us to come up and sing. All four of us went to the front of the room, and after several false starts, we settled down with a barbershop rendition of "I've Been Working on the Railroad." We followed up with "Down by the Old Mill Stream." Then, all the exuberant cheering and clapping encouraged us to sing an encore. So, we gave them "Jingle Bells." It was a comical scene. "Jingle Bells" presented to a Chinese soldier audience in the middle of the Malayan jungle by four tattered American Airmen.

We relaxed for several days in this new camp. Yung Han and the soldiers in his garrison were friendly, and they fed us well. It gave us time to revitalize.

But one day, everything changed for the worse.

February 1st, our 19th day in the jungle, was a day none of us will ever forget. It was the day jungle fever struck. Duffy came down with it first, and then Hansman. Duffy would survive, but Hansman would end up in an unmarked grave deep in the life-taking Malayan jungle.

We had no way of knowing what the fever was. Saltzman and I were untouched by it, but Duff and Hansman became worse every day. Night and day, they burned with fever and shook with chills. Most of the time, they were delirious. Saltz and I watched them as they fought our last battle in the *Postville Express* against the Japanese Zeros over and over in their hallucinations caused by the fever.

I went to Yung Han and asked what he could do for Hansman and Duffy. He came to our basha, looked at them, and left. He came back five minutes later with a large, green bottle that looked like a quart bottle of 7-Up. Yung Han shook it, took a drink of the contents, and handed the bottle to me. He motioned for me to take a drink. It was a vile tasting white liquid that puckered my mouth. Yung Han then motioned for Duff and Hansman to take a slug. They each took a drink and threw it up. Saltzman took a slug and kept it down. Yung Han handed the bottle back to me, and this slug was just as sour as the first one, very bitter. My mouth puckered again, but it stayed down. Saltzman took a second drink, and it stayed down. Yung Han looked pleased. Then Duff and Hansman took another slug, but they both threw it up. Yung Han shook his head in disappointment, handed me the bottle, and left.

When Bartholomew returned, he said it was quinine water in the bottle, which would cure malaria. He said we must drink the quinine water every morning and every evening.

Bartholomew told us about the Cinchona tree that grew wild in the jungle. The natives searched in the rainforest until they found one and then tapped it just like they tapped a rubber tree. They collected the sap in a bottle, and that was what we were drinking. The problem was, only Saltzman and I could keep it down, and Duff and Hansman, who needed it, could not.

That night Duffy and Hansman were on their jungle beds, out of their minds and moaning and screaming in agony. I noticed a few Communist guerrillas giggling, chattering, and laughing as they watched the two men suffer from the fever. Years of intense hatred for the British resulted in their distrust and icy contempt for all white men. They were enjoying the misery that Duff and Hansman were experiencing.

Duff and Hansman got sicker and sicker. They could not keep the quinine water remedy down, so their fever went way up each night. They would run off into the jungle, screaming out of their minds.

Saltzman and I would chase after them to bring them back to the basha. We ended up tying them down with rattan. When the fever went down, they would shake so hard that the whole basha shook. After a while, they quieted down, and we tried again to make them drink the quinine water. They still could not keep it down.

After several days of asking Yung Han to find more help, I lost my temper. I went to Yung Han's basha and demanded that he send men out to search for a doctor who had more medicine. He agreed and said if I wrote a letter, he would have it delivered to an Indian physician living at a rubber plantation in a Japanese-occupied town 20 miles away. I wrote the letter that day, describing as best I could the symptoms of Duff's and Hansman's illness. A native guerrilla left with it that night. Three days later, he returned, but stomach pills were the only medications he brought back. They were of no benefit to either Duff or Hansman.

The next day, another runner arrived with a letter from the Indian doctor. It said if the two well Americans—Saltzman and I—came to see him, he would give us medicine for the men who were ill. Saltz and I thought it might be a trap because the doctor lived near a Japanese-occupied town. After some deliberation, we took the chance and made the 20-mile journey.

We left that morning with Yung Han as a guide and Bartholomew and three Chinese armed with rifles. Yung Han left his junior commanding officer in charge at the Anti-Jap Army Regiment outpost, instructing him to watch over Duffy and Hansman. We walked all day through the rough jungle trails, and as it got dark, we made it to English Tom's small Communist outpost in the middle of the jungle close to the doctor's house. When we arrived, we found a letter waiting for us from the Communist Anti-Jap Headquarters Commander. It ordered the two of us, probably because we were not sick, to proceed to another guerrilla camp to begin arrangements for our escape from Malaya. We did not know what to do at first because Hansman and Duff were so sick. But after some intense deliberation, Saltzman and I went. We needed to find a way out of the jungle or all of us would soon die there. But first, we needed to stop by the Indian doctor's house on the plantation to pick up the medicine for Hansman and Duffy.

We arrived at the rubber plantation just after dark and saw no other human beings anywhere. Our guerrilla bodyguards appeared worried about going farther into the plantation to the doctor's house because the Japanese operated the plantation, and pro-Jap coolies were all around the area. Yung Han ordered the bodyguards to keep moving, so we headed down a row of rubber trees. We stopped for a minute to look around, and when we did not see anybody, one of the guerrilla guides led us up a paved road to the front of a small wooden house set back in a clearing on the edge of the rubber plantation. Our guide went back into the rubber trees to wait with the others.

We knocked on the door, and a tall, slender Indian man opened it and invited Saltz and me into his home. The doctor spoke excellent English and said he was the doctor for this large rubber plantation where he also lived. He asked us to take a seat at his dining table in the middle of the front room and then disappeared into an adjoining room. He returned with a bottle of Johnny Walker Black Label Scotch and three glasses and poured each of us a two-finger drink. Then he opened with a statement. "All white men who come to the jungle get malaria." With that said, he told us he received his medical training in his native country, India, and moved to Malaya to work on this rubber plantation.

As we sipped our Scotch, which was a pleasant surprise to our lips, we described Duff's and Hansman's illness in as much detail as we could. After we finished, he looked down, rubbed his brown head, and contemplated his diagnosis. After a while, he looked up and said he thought the boys were suffering from malaria or cholera or both. He gave us a bottle of quinine water and several small bottles of something he called cholera mix. I read the label on one of the bottles of cholera mix, and the remedy list was long. It included cholera, morning sickness, backache, and eight to 10 other things. The doctor explained that the cholera mix would help them keep the quinine water down.

We enjoyed a wonderful meal of curried chicken and rice. The doctor made it clear that he only cooked with curry that came from his homeland, India. It was a pleasurable experience after the jungle fare we had been eating. When we finished dinner, we stood up and thanked our host for his exceptional hospitality.

As we were leaving, the doctor said, "You wait here. I will go out ahead of you to check the path to ensure the area is clear for you to leave." He opened the door to check and quickly closed it again. In a whispered voice, he said, "There is a Japanese patrol coming up the path. Go out the back door, wait for my signal, and then run. I will say the word *well* in a loud voice. That is your signal to run."

We slipped out the back door and waited for the signal. The Japanese patrol knocked at the front door. The doctor opened the door and welcomed a Japanese officer accompanied by two soldiers. From what we could understand, the Colonel had a severe blister on one of his legs and wanted the doctor to look at it. The doctor took the officer into his operating room, and then, with an emphatic voice, the doctor said, "Well." Saltzman and I left from the back of the house and snuck down the path. Two Jap soldiers were on the front porch joking and smoking, but they never knew we were there just 50 feet away. After we crossed the road, we walked farther into the trees where we found Yung Han, Bartholomew, and our three Chinese bodyguards waiting for us.

We made our way back to Lowe-Shin's outpost with the medicine for Duffy and Hansman. When we arrived, we found a Communist guerrilla from Communist Headquarters waiting for us. The guerrilla said he was there to escort us to the next camp.

We sent one of our Chinese bodyguards back to Yung Han's regiment outpost with the medicine for Duff and Hansman with the following note.

Dear Duff and Hansman,

We met with the doctor, and he believes you are suffering from malaria and cholera. Take the quinine water and cholera mixture accompanying our note.

We arrived at Lowe-Shin's and received word from Communist HQ. It instructs us to go to HQ to begin arrangements to depart from Malaya. Saltz and I have proceeded as directed. We hope to see you as soon as you can travel.

Hump

We thought the medications would help Duff and Hansman, so we headed out with the Communist guerrilla escort to the Communist Headquarters where we hoped to find a radio to contact the Allies and plan an escape out of the jungle for the four of us.

Besides our new guerrilla guide, the group for this trip included Yung Han and his interpreter Lowe-Shin (English Tom), our two remaining Chinese guards, Bartholomew, Saltzman, and me. We began the journey walking through rows of rubber trees and then jungle brush for three hours. Along the way, we saw a massive four-foot-wide stream of ants traveling along the floor of the rainforest. The broad line of ants stretched for hundreds of yards before disappearing into large holes in the earth. There must have been millions of them intent on their task, whatever that was. They were just one of many wonderments of the jungle we would experience.

As we approached a massive camp, my first thought was, "This must be the Supreme Headquarters of the Communist Anti-Japanese Army." But it turned out it was only a Third Regiment outpost of the Anti-Jap Army, and they did not have a radio. Since this larger 50-guerrilla garrison was so deep in the jungle, we thought it would be a safe place away from the Japanese soldiers. We would soon find out we were far from safe. The tenacious Japanese soldiers were not giving up their search for the downed B-29 Airmen they hated with a vengeance.

Almost as soon as we arrived, Yung Han told us that for some unknown reason, the Communist Anti-Jap Army had delayed our journey to the Supreme Headquarters. He said we would wait at this Third Regiment outpost until we received further instructions.

After several days of sitting and waiting, English Tom came to our basha. He told us a Malay native village near his small outpost invited us to a dinner party, and we accepted.

Saltzman and I left around noon with English Tom and two armed guerrilla guides. After walking three hours through the jungle along animal trails and rows of rubber trees, we arrived at English Tom's small camp in the middle of the afternoon. The Malay natives gave us some rice to eat and told us we must keep moving because the village natives expected us to be at their village for the party by early evening. English Tom wanted to stay there at his home, so we bid him farewell and continued with our two guides to reach our dinner party on time.

It was raining when we left, and we walked in the rain until around 5:00 p.m. when the downpour changed to a drizzle. As the rain stopped, we came out of the bush into a rubber plantation where newly planted rubber trees in neat rows stretched for miles.

At the end of the rubber tree fields were several houses on stilts. All the people were waving and happy to see us as we passed by. They seemed to know we were coming. At first, that worried me, always alert for a Japanese ambush, but we arrived safely at the village with 15 or 20 native houses, and the dinner party began.

The Malay natives came running out to welcome us. The men laid an eight-foot-by-eight-foot woven mat on the open ground in the center of the village. It looked like a village square. Some Malay native boys brought out two chairs and placed them on the mat for us to sit on. Saltzman and I sat down, and we were the center of attention. All eyes were on us.

One native who came forward out of the group wore semi-pressed khaki pants and a white semi-pressed button-down shirt. He was taller than the rest, had a very slim build, and was well-groomed. His dark black hair was greased and combed off to one side. He introduced himself in English as M. Pilas and said he was a civil servant before the Japanese arrived in early 1942. He would be our interpreter for the evening festivities.

The natives gathered and sat all around us, but nobody sat on the woven mat. It seemed they laid it out just for us as their special guests. Several young Malay ladies came dashing out of nearby houses dressed in colorful, long dresses and served us tea and sugar cakes. The Malay men were dressed in an assortment of styles, a mishmash of clothes picked up from the British. They asked us many questions about the B-29s. They also wanted to know about the progress of the war. M. Pilas interpreted for the crowd of Malays who numbered about 50.

Then M. Pilas stood up, took a few steps back from the group, and began telling us about the nearby rubber plantation and how the natives tapped the trees every morning. Each day, the tapped latex sap ran down a small, wooden spout into a small cup. The natives collected the sap from the cups each afternoon and took the buckets filled with the liquid to a central area where they poured it into wooden flats. The final product was a latex rubber sheet about three feet wide, five feet long, and a quarter-inch thick after it dried in each flat. Everybody in this village worked on the Japanese-controlled plantation, but nobody ever talked about the Japanese while we were there.

Just before dark, they served everyone hot rice, curried chicken, cold rice flour cakes, and tea. We were the only two people allowed to sit on the mat for dinner. All the Malay natives circled the mat as they ate their dinner. M. Pilas told us these natives appreciated the American B-29 Airmen who helped them in the war against the Japanese. They wanted to show us their gratitude.

After dinner, to thank our new friends for their hospitality, we sang the Army Air Corps song for them. Soon after dark, Saltz and I departed to go back to the Third Regiment Anti-Jap Army outpost. As we left, a Malay boy honored us with two live ducks and a chicken as a gift to thank us for coming to visit their village.

We walked close to 20 miles in the steaming jungle for one little dinner party. But we enjoyed a lovely time with a group of grateful and cordial Malay natives. It became clear how much these natives wanted the war to end and the Japanese out of their country.

During the long walk back to our camp from the dinner party, one of our guides stopped us at a rather large house along the road. There was no light anywhere. The home was dark, both inside and out. Then, with no apprehension, our guide walked up a path and knocked on the door. The door cracked open, and our guide talked with the occupant in Chinese. We soon found out he was our guide's friend. Now speaking English, the man invited us inside his dark house, lit a lamp, and introduced himself. Our new friend was an educated middle-aged Chinese man who was friendly with the Chinese Communist Party and the Communist guerrillas. He spoke excellent English.

Our new friend said there were no Japanese in the area because they had already left by that time of night. The Chinese prearranged with our guide, his friend, to stop by because he wanted to meet us, and he wanted to know the truth about how the war was going. He asked us to move to the back of the room and sit at a table while the two guerrilla guides guarded the door outside. On the table were stalks of bananas of many kinds. He asked us to enjoy the bananas while he made a fresh pot of hot coffee. It was a welcome rest on our long journey back to camp from the party. He talked about how terrible the Japanese were and how he wished the Allies would soon defeat them. He asked many questions about the Allied Forces and our American home. We stayed with our Chinese friend for about an hour, and during this brief visit, we ate lots of bananas—regular yellow bananas, smaller ripe green ones, pink ones, purple ones, red ones. There were all sizes, from standard to small finger size. There were at least 10 different varieties and sizes. The small reddish ones had a nutty flavor and were delicious. Saltz must have eaten 30 of the red nutty ones.

Once Saltzman filled himself with small red bananas, we were ready to continue our long walk through the jungle back to the Third Regiment outpost. Our new Chinese friend turned out the lamp and went to the door to ask our guerrilla guides to look around to ensure it was safe for us to leave. As we left, he thanked us for visiting him and asked us to come back for dinner three nights later. We did not know we would never keep that dinner appointment.

We arrived back at our camp at 1:00 in the morning, exhausted, and hit the sack.

CHAPTER 7

Sakai

The next day, Yung Han informed us he had received a message instructing us to leave to go to a camp farther into the jungle. The Japs were closing in on us in this area, and it was now too dangerous for us. Yung Han explained to Bartholomew that he should tell us it would be a long, challenging walk of several days through a very rough part of the jungle, and we should try to get some rest.

Yung Han received orders to stay with the Third Regiment outpost. Early the next morning, we left with only young Bartholomew and two guides with rifles. We walked all morning on animal trails through the dense jungle. The guerrillas stopped at noon and somehow built a fire in the pouring rain to boil tea for lunch. We all drank hot tea and ate cold, precooked rice. Then we continued walking all afternoon until 5:00 p.m. when the guides stopped on the bank of a small, shallow stream. Saltzman and I were both exhausted from the journey, so we sat down on the stream bank to rest and talk to Bartholomew. He was an intelligent young man. It was disheartening for me to know the Communist Party was brainwashing him to mold him into one of their future Party leaders.

The guides decided our home base for the night should be alongside the stream bed and got busy cutting down small trees with their machetes to build bashas for us for the night. They pounded several stakes into the ground until the tops of the stakes were about two feet off the ground. The Chinese intertwined and fastened saplings to the top of the stakes with rattan strips they cut from the jungle. Bartholomew said they were building the sapling bed two feet off the ground to keep the centipedes, snakes, and other jungle beasts from sleeping with us during the night. Next, they fastened six-foot poles to the front stakes of the sapling beds and shorter four-foot poles to the back stakes to make a basha frame that would slant from the front to the rear. They cut more small saplings to secure a structure for the roof. After they cut down several large palm leaves to build the roof, they started at the bottom and moved to the top, layering the palm leaves into a waterproof cover. This basha construction took them only 20 to 30 minutes. We were soon lying on our sapling beds two feet above the ground under waterproof roofs.

After completing the bashas, the guides built a fire and started making our usual meal—rice. We were surprised to see an addition to our menu. One of the guides had disappeared into the jungle and came back with what looked like vines from sweet potato plants. The green vines looked like spinach to us, so we called them our jungle spinach from then on.

We ate hot rice and jungle spinach and then laid down to sleep in our quick but well-constructed bashas. The guides kept putting wood on the fire to keep it flaming enough so, according to Bartholomew, the Bengal tigers would not bother us during the night. We could hear elephants trumpeting all around us. Bartholomew said they were telling us to leave their territory. Saltzman and I were so tired we did not question the comfort of our beds. Not even tigers or trumpeting elephants could keep us awake.

The next morning at dawn, we left and walked three more days through the wet, dense Malayan jungle, only stopping each evening to build a basha and eat rice and jungle spinach. These three days were long with challenging terrain. We needed rest and a good meal.

On the afternoon of the third day, we walked into a large clearing dotted with gigantic, unusual looking trees. The bases of the trees were 30 to 40 feet in circumference, and extensive roots sprouted out from the sides of the tree trunks at 15 feet above the ground. These roots fanned out and entered back into the ground 20 to 25 feet from the base of the main tree trunk. These trees were monstrous. The natives cut off several of the enormous trunks at about 30 feet above the ground and constructed square bamboo huts with palm leaf roofs on the flat cut-off trunk surfaces. The flat tops of these gigantic tree stumps were still 20 feet across. They built each square hut larger in depth and width than its round tree trunk foundation. The sides of the square structure extended several feet beyond the edge of the round trunk.

Bartholomew later told us the natives built the huts on top of these giant tree trunks so the elephants could not push them over or damage them. He said the elephants were territorial, and they had already destroyed the bashas the guerrillas built for us each night on our walk here. Bartholomew told us that after we left camp each morning, the elephants came, pushed over the bashas, and trampled them into the ground. The natives built their homes 30 feet in the air on the enormous tree trunks, away from the elephants' reach.

As we walked farther into the clearing, two short, dark-skinned men came walking toward us. One had a huge goiter. They were around four feet six inches tall and wore only loincloths with no shirts or shoes. They approached us with a nonaggressive demeanor and appeared to be harmless. Bartholomew, who spoke Chinese, English, and Malay, tried to talk to them but could not communicate. We all stood looking at each other for a minute, and then the native with the goiter started motioning with his hands for us to sit down on a nearby log.

Our new friends turned and walked away, leaving us sitting on the log. After a few minutes, they returned with a young man around 20 years of age who looked just like his two companions. He started talking to Saltzman and me in Malay. After he realized we did not understand, he tried conversing with Bartholomew. Bartholomew understood and told the young man we were the characters who flew over their villages in the enormous birds in the sky.

Bartholomew turned back to us to explain that we were in a Sakai village. He told us the Sakai were aborigine natives who have lived in the jungle all their lives and never leave their jungle home. They have never left their native environment and have never seen a white man before us. Bartholomew said this young man could speak some Malay because he was the only one designated by the tribe to go to the village to trade ivory for salt. For the Sakai, salt was scarce. The only available salt was the small amount from animal licks in the jungle.

Because of the lack of salt in their diets, almost all the men and women had goiters. The Sakai gathered ivory tusks from elephant graveyards. Then this young man took the ivory to a nearby village to trade it for salt. Over the years, while negotiating and selling the ivory for salt, the young man learned to speak Malay.

Bartholomew talked with the young man about our need to cross the swampland lake, Tasek Bera, to the Communist guerrilla camp on the other side. The young man told Bartholomew he would speak with the Sakai Chief, and after he received permission, he and some others would help us cross the Tasek Bera.

The young Sakai motioned for us to follow him and led us to one of the cut-off trees with a bamboo hut on top. Bartholomew said he wanted us to climb the rattan ladder up to the Sakai house on top of the stump and wait there until they returned for us.

We climbed the 30-foot ladder, went through a small hole at the top, and crawled into the hut. We looked around and were surprised when we saw a monkey staring at us. The pet monkey, tied to a long leash, was sitting on the ledge of one of the open windows.

At the other end of the hut, a man was sitting on the floor in the corner. He was an older man with a large goiter, and it seemed like he might be the owner of the hut. He looked at the two of us who had just invaded his home, but he appeared disinterested. The monkey studied us for a minute and then jumped down and ran to his owner.

There was no furniture. We sat on the floor made of bamboo trees tied together with rattan strips. The bamboo was about two or three inches in diameter with a small space between each one. We learned later that this space was there for disposal. Everything they pushed through and what fell through the gaps went to the animals below. The hut was square with four sturdy bamboo walls and three open-air square windows with no coverings.

It was awkward. The man and his monkey were in this small room with us, but we could not talk to him, and he could not communicate with us. He just sat there chewing his betel nut with red saliva running down the sides of his mouth onto his chin. After several minutes, the monkey became agitated and began to scamper around the small one-room hut while still tied to his leash.

The man's only clothing was a loincloth and a rattan belt tied around his waist with several small leather pouches attached on each side. As we sat watching, the Sakai native reached into one of the leather pouches to find a roll of what looked like cigarette paper so thin you could see through it. He ripped off a small square piece of paper from the roll. Out of another pouch, he poured what looked like tobacco into the piece of paper, rolled it into a perfect cigarette, and then licked it like a Western cowboy to seal it.

After putting the cigarette between his lips on the side of his mouth, he went to another pouch and took out a small piece of ivory about four inches long and three-quarters of an inch thick with a dowel in the center. He took the dowel out of the ivory and licked the end. Next, reaching into a pouch, he pulled out some punk and put it on the dowel. Then he inserted the dowel back into the hole in the ivory and hit it with his fist. When he pulled it right back out, and the punk was on fire. After blowing on it to fan the flame, he used it to light his cigarette. I sat there in amazement watching this whole process.

Saltzman, an aeronautical engineer, said the dowel's compression into the ivory caused the punk to light. He said it was like the compression of a diesel engine cylinder igniting the fuel in a diesel motor. It seemed like the man understood everything Saltz said because I thought I saw a flicker of proud acknowledgment on the man's face as he listened. The Sakai's small feat of ingenuity was astonishing from an aborigine who had never left the jungle and had never been in touch with any outside civilization.

Then the Sakai gentleman called his monkey over to his side to calm him down, and they sat together studying us while he enjoyed his cigarette. We would soon find out our new silent friend was the head man and leader of this Sakai village.

Bartholomew soon came shouting at us to come down from the hut to join him. He led us to the Sakai village center where we all sat down on a large log surrounded by several other smaller logs that formed a semi-circle. It looked like the Sakai had dragged the logs to this location years ago. The logs to sit on and a nearby fire pit for cooking made it seem like it was all set up for their tribal gatherings.

Bartholomew said again that this was the first time the Sakai had ever seen a white man. And even better, we were the white men who could fly those enormous birds. So it thrilled them to have us as guests. They were going to give us a big welcoming party to honor us.

After we sat talking for a while, the Sakai started coming from all directions down the many worn dirt paths to join us. The Sakai did not dress up for our welcoming party. They all came barefooted, wearing nothing but a loincloth. It also appeared that all the men and women had goiters.

One young man came running toward us with a big smile on his face and a live goat slung over his shoulders. He stopped about 15 feet away, threw down the young goat to the ground, slit its throat, and skinned it. He erected a spit over the fire pit to cook the goat, built a fire, and in just minutes, the goat was spinning on the spit.

A young lady around 17 years old arrived with nothing on but a skimpy loincloth and a baby strapped across her back. She took some nuts from the handwoven basket she carried and, with a big smile, offered a handful of nuts to Saltzman. He smiled, thanked the young native Sakai girl, and said, "Hump, I think I like these new Sakai friends of ours."

More Sakai men and women soon came with loads of pineapples, papaya, bananas, ducks, pheasants, and a mouse deer. They all started preparing the meal on separate smaller fires while our main course, the goat, turned on a spit over the big fire. As I sat watching the Sakai prepare for the festivities, I thought, "This will be one shindig I will never forget."

No one other than Bartholomew could understand us when we spoke, and none of the Sakai could understand what Bartholomew was saying except for the young man who traded the ivory for salt. So, there was not a lot of conversation at the dinner party.

Even though their ancestors were from the head-hunter tribes in Borneo, they were friendly to us. We wanted to tell them about the war and the B-29s, but since we could not communicate, everyone just sat around, ate, and smiled. There were lots of laughs and lots of smiles.

We all enjoyed a wonderful meal, and just before dusk, all the Sakai gathered everything until the clearing was neat and clean. Then they wandered off to their huts or into the jungle somewhere. The Sakai who spoke Malay left word with Bartholomew to tell us which one of their bamboo huts on top of the tree trunks we were to sleep in that night.

Bartholomew said they arranged it with our silent friend, the Sakai leader of the village, for the Sakai to paddle us in dugouts across the Tasek Bera to a location on the other side where we could continue to the Communist camp. He said the Japs would not follow us through the Tasek Bera swampland. He also said we would not be ready to leave for at least another day because he needed more time to complete the arrangements for the dugout canoes, and the Chief had not decided which Sakai would be our guides.

The next morning, the young Sakai told Bartholomew he wanted to take us fishing. The young Sakai had just traded some ivory for a large metal wok, and the tribe was eager to show it off and put it to good use.

We soon headed out on our fishing trip. Two of the Sakai led the way, proudly carrying their prized wok. They tied the wok to a bamboo pole with the ends of the bamboo resting on each of their shoulders and started down a trail. Following behind the proud wok bearers were several other Sakai men carrying heavy, wooden, hand-carved bats about four feet long. Behind them were eight women, all holding large handwoven baskets on their heads. Bartholomew, Saltzman, and I were on another new adventure.

After walking several miles, we stopped in front of a large, different looking tree that stood out from the rest. The Sakai walked around the trunk several times, checking the tree. After several minutes of discussion, they took the hand-carved bats and started beating on the tree. They banged on the trunk and the lower limbs until the wood was soft and the sap ran out. Then one of the young men took half of a hollowed-out coconut and collected the seeping fluid into the shell.

They repeated this process several times, and after two hours of beating on this tree and gathering the sap, the coconut shell was about half full. The Sakai huddled in a circle, and after a lengthy discussion and when everybody seemed satisfied, we returned to the trail. We walked a mile or more into the jungle and then stopped at the shore of a vast and shallow river. The river was about 100 yards wide, but the water was only a foot or two deep. After the Sakai stood on the bank for a while, surmising the conditions and discussing strategy, two men took the coconut shell with the tree sap and walked upstream. The others built a wooden cradle for the new wok and started a good-sized fire under it. They poured some coconut oil from several leather pouches into the wok to heat it for cooking.

The ladies motioned for Bartholomew, Saltzman, and me to follow them into the river and then handed each of us a half-a-bushel-sized handwoven rattan basket. We lined up with the women across the river, all holding a basket. The men with the coconut shell full of sap from the tree were several hundred yards upstream. They poured the sap across the river in several places, and minutes later, hundreds of fish of all sizes came to the surface and floated downstream. Everyone with a basket started scooping up fish. The young Sakai men carried the full bamboo baskets of fish over to the riverbank and poured the fish into the hot coconut oil in the wok. After a few minutes, they removed the French-fried fish and reloaded the wok with more fresh fish. There were soon several baskets full of fried fish, just caught out of the jungle stream and ready to eat. Everyone sat down and enjoyed a delightful tasting fried fish lunch. As we were eating our fish lunch, the young Sakai asked Bartholomew if we would like to see how they used their blowguns for hunting. Bartholomew asked us if we had any interest in a hunting trip with blowguns.

Saltz said, "Hump, I'm game if you are."

I said, "Hunting! Blowguns! Let's go!"

After lunch, they gave us a lesson on how they hunted in the jungle with blowguns. A few of the elder Sakai who carried long bamboo blowguns took Bartholomew, Saltzman, me, and the young Sakai down some animal paths away from the group at the stream. We stopped in an area where monkeys were scampering around everywhere in the trees. We watched as the Sakai showed how they used blowguns and poison darts for hunting animals. They dipped some darts in curare, a poison mixture they stored in their pouches. Each Sakai elder placed a dart in his blowgun and put the blowgun in his mouth. Using their hands, they aimed the blowguns up toward the trees. They blew the darts into two monkeys in the trees about 50 feet away. Seconds later, after shaking in the tree a bit, the monkeys fell and lay dead on the ground. The men were extremely accurate with the blowguns, and the poison darts were deadly. That was a hunting trip I will never forget.

The next day, we left for the Communist Headquarters on the other side of the Tasek Bera swampland. We moved away from the

Japanese Army into a safer territory where we hoped to find a much-needed radio.

Two Sakai men led Saltz and me to the edge of the large Tasek Bera swampland lake, where we found two hand-hewn dugouts tied to the shoreline trees and waiting for us. The Sakai jumped right into the back of each dugout and motioned for us to get in. Saltzman jumped down into his dugout in front of his Sakai guide. But I had more trouble getting in with my long legs. As I squeezed into the bottom of my dugout, not made for large people like me, the water lapped over the edge on both sides. It didn't seem to bother our Sakai boatmen as they paddled us off into the wilderness of the jungle swampland lake.

Bartholomew and our Chinese guides did not come with us on this trip. We left to cross this swampland lake with two Sakai natives we did not know and who could not speak English. We did not know where we were going or how far. The moss-filled tree limbs and vines hung down from above as we weaved through the swampland maze. Snakes hung from the tree limbs all along the way. Beautiful multicolored birds watched as we floated beneath them. We could not move a muscle because with the slightest movement, water came over the sides of the dugout. I wondered what would happen if one of those snakes dropped out of the trees into my lap.

As we looked down into the clear water, we could see all kinds of fish following the boats, but all we could think of was the possibility of piranha or other man-eating types of fish or snakes that might lurk beneath us.

I became very stiff from sitting still for so long crammed into the bottom of the small dugout. It became dark early, and many questions popped into my mind since I could no longer see my surroundings. I could not turn around to look at my guide, so I just looked ahead into the darkness and hoped this ordeal would end soon with me not at the bottom of the lake.

We traveled on the lake for two more hours when at last we reached the other side. I could barely move my cramped legs as I climbed out onto the land. Saltzman's dugout landed right after mine, and we discussed how thankful we were to be on the semi-dry ground again out of that fearful mess. As we walked around to loosen up our muscles and stretch after the long trip in the cramped dugouts, two armed Chinese guerrillas came walking through the jungle swamp to meet us.

They motioned for us to follow them. I turned to thank the Sakai, but they and their dugouts were already long gone, swallowed up in the dark Tasek Bera swamp. How our new guides knew when and where we would arrive we did not know, but the jungle telegraph system continued to work its wonders.

CHAPTER 8

Woo-Ping

We walked for two more miserable and horrific hours through thick jungle brush and swampland water sometimes up to our necks. After surviving the Tasek Bera crossing and two more hours of the swamp, we came to the guerrilla camp that we again thought was the Anti-Jap Army Headquarters. When we first arrived, Saltz said, "Hump, I think this is it. I think we made it to Supreme Military Headquarters."

"I hope you are right, Saltz. And I hope they have a radio."

The camp's strategic location on the shores of the Tasek Bera with a large garrison of more than 100 guerrillas made us think it could be the Supreme Headquarters of the Communist Anti-Jap Army. It looked like the soldiers were well-armed. I even saw a few of the guerrillas holding Bren machine guns. The British abandoned many of those in the jungle when they fled Malaya in 1942.

Had we reached the Supreme Military Headquarters where there was a radio to message Allied Headquarters for help? It seemed too good to be true. It turned out it was too good to be true. This camp was only a Third Regiment Anti-Jap Army middle post, and again, there was no radio.

But this new guerrilla camp was a well-planned site compared to the other Communist outposts we had passed through before. There were only two rough and swampy ways to get into this camp, and guerrillas with Bren machine guns covered both ways. Otherwise, untouched jungle and deep swamp surrounded the campsite. I felt like the surroundings here would keep us safe from the Japanese.

The day we arrived, to our surprise, there were two men we already knew stationed at this garrison post—Yung Han and his interpreter, the Chinese we called English Tom. The Anti-Jap Army transferred Yung Han from the other Third Regiment outpost, and he now commanded this middle outpost of the Third Regiment. We last saw English Tom several weeks ago. He was always full of news that came through the Chinese grapevine.

"English Tom, do you have any news for us?" I asked.

English Tom answered, "I heard the Americans are now taking over the Philippine Islands, and more B-29s out of the 20th Bomber Command are bombing Singapore." This news made us feel like the war was nearing an end.

"English Tom," I asked, "have you heard anything about the rest of my crew members? Any news of their whereabouts?"

"No, sorry, still no news of any other American Airmen."

Then they showed us to a small basha that would be our home for a while. We were encouraged to hear the news about the Allies' success in the Philippines and the B-29 bombing raids. But I was discouraged

106

by the unknown whereabouts of my crew, still not knowing who made it and who didn't. We settled ourselves into our new home and hit the sack for some much-needed rest.

The day after our arrival, several Chinese Communist guerrillas stationed at this garrison asked us to join them in a game. We accepted their invitation and followed them into the campsite clearing. We did not know what to expect. It turned out to be an ordinary game of tag with some boundary lines they drew in the dirt on each side of the clearing. One of the Chinese said he learned the game in an English missionary school as a child. We played for two hours, and the Chinese were having a great time whooping and screaming like kids. Imagine the scene—a dozen murderous looking Chinese guerrillas, all heavily armed, playing tag with two tattered American Airmen in a military camp deep in the Malayan jungle.

That was the last fun we enjoyed in this camp. The next morning, we woke up early when we heard three loud blasts of a whistle. It was the signal for a Regimental assembly of the guerrillas. The Chinese took off like scalded dogs to gather their equipment and get into formation in the clearing. Even the kitchen boys rushed to fall in line.

We walked out to watch as the Third Regiment garrison scrambled to finish forming several straight lines. Then a young Chinese with three stars on his cap and a sports shirt with epaulets sewn on the shoulders, followed by seven soldiers, marched in a parade-like fashion into the clearing, stopping in the front of the guerrillas' formation. The young Chinese wore jodhpurs and leggings with blue and white trim and carried a British revolver on a blue lanyard. He was the new Number One Captain assigned to the Third Regiment Anti-Jap Army middle post. He was the first Chinese guerrilla we had seen who looked like a Chinese Anti-Jap Army Commanding Officer.

Without even a glance at us, the new Number One Captain walked up and down the lines of men in formation, bawling out one here and one there for not holding his rifle in the correct position or some other small Army detail. He walked to the front of the formation, made a brief speech, and dismissed the garrison. Yung Han greeted the new commander and escorted him to the largest basha in the camp. His name was Woo-Ping, and everyone seemed to fear him. His reputation preceded him.

About 8:00 that night, we were sitting on the sapling bed in our basha when English Tom rushed in to tell us to come to Woo-Ping's basha for dinner. We hurried over, both excited and surprised the new chief invited us to dinner. We looked forward to having the chance to talk with him. But it shocked us when we entered his basha and saw the setup.

At one end of the table sat Woo-Ping, Yung Han, and English Tom. In front of them was a steaming pot of chicken. At the other end of the table were two places set for Saltzman and me, but there was only a small bowl of thin rice gruel in front of each of our settings.

Averting his eyes and ashamed, English Tom showed us to our seats. Woo-Ping paid no attention to us. He just sat there sipping on something for a few minutes and then started eating chicken and drinking his coffee. We sat there watching and drank our gruel. Woo-Ping ate until the pot was empty.

For the next half hour, Woo-Ping told us how the Red Army was progressing and how the Americans were not. Saltzman and I brought up the subject of our situation. We told him we wanted to go to the Communists' Supreme Military Headquarters because we thought a radio transmitter might be there that we could use to contact the Allies and arrange our escape from Malaya. Woo-Ping said we could not go until we wrote a letter to the Central Military Committee at Supreme Headquarters asking permission.

We explained we had already done that once while in another guerrilla camp commanded by the one we called Hollywood. He said Hollywood did not matter to him and we needed to write another letter asking for permission. With that, he stood up and motioned for us to leave his basha.

The next morning, Saltz and I were playing cards when English Tom came to tell us that Woo-Ping wanted to see us. When we arrived at his basha, Woo-Ping was sitting at a table looking over some propaganda newspapers and did not acknowledge our arrival for 10 minutes. Then he looked up with a cold and unfriendly demeanor and asked us, "Is Russia good or bad?"

This out-of-the-blue question thrown at us by a Chinese guerrilla in the middle of the Malayan jungle knocked us off balance. I stammered a bit and said our country considered Russia its ally in this war. Woo-Ping shrugged his shoulders, indicating that he thought my answer did not show proper respect for Russia.

There were about a hundred small pamphlets on the table in front of him. I could never get my hands on one to read it, but because there were Soviet hammer and sickle symbols on the covers, I could guess the nature of the contents. Besides the pamphlets, there was also an eye-catching, four-inch-thick book with a cherry-red book cover on the table. When I asked him what it was, he said it was a Russian manual on guerrilla warfare tactics. I was wondering where he got such a manual. When I picked it up, he called our attention to a world atlas on the table. Woo-Ping slid it in front of him and flipped the pages to a map of the United States. Then he demanded that we show him where each of us lived. I pointed at northeastern Iowa, and Saltzman pointed at Washington, DC. I then pointed at Chicago, Duffy's home, and for the first time, Woo-Ping looked interested. He perked up in his chair and said Chicago was a proper city because many Communists lived there.

Woo-Ping bragged about what the Communist movement was going to do for Malaya after the war. He said liberating Malaya meant freedom from the British and the Japanese. The Communists would see that everyone received an excellent education and the chance to make a living wage. He boasted that he received six years of free schooling, and after the war when they were in charge, the Communists would see that everyone in all Malaya received free education. Then he asked us if American democracy could offer as much. It was difficult not to laugh at his arrogant attitude and ignorance, but I told him with a calm voice that we received 12 years of free education, and in the United States, that was common practice and the law. He first showed his surprise and then became angry because we had topped him.

Woo-Ping did not like white men because the Englishmen who ran the country of Malaya as a British Crown Colony had oppressed the Chinese for many years. Britain controlled most of Malaya for more than 60 years. The Japanese invaded the British and Australian bases in Northern Malaya just hours before they bombed Pearl Harbor in December 1941. When the British surrendered to Japan on February 15, 1945, the Japanese occupied the Malay Peninsula and Singapore, and everything changed.

Although Woo-Ping knew we were Americans, he still associated us with the British, and his dislike for us had been evident the evening of the first day he strode into camp. We were always mindful that we depended on the Chinese and Woo-Ping for our lives and needed their help with our escape from the Malayan jungle. He could shoot us and bury us in the remote rainforest, and no one would ever hear of us again. To one of these Chinese guerrillas like Woo-Ping, snuffing out human life, a white human life, was like stepping on an ant. Perhaps it was a blessing from God because despite their disdain for us, the Chinese continued to help us.

In the days that followed, Woo-Ping proved to be a ruthless commander. He would drill his malnourished garrison up and down the clearing, parading them for hours in the searing heat and humidity, never allowing them to drink water. He watched them as he lounged in the shade of his basha, drinking tea and smoking cigarettes. These men were his Army troops, and he treated them like they were prisoners of war.

Woo-Ping continued to give us a working example of the Communism he practiced. He stated to us many times during several of his propaganda rants that in the Communist Army, every man was equal and shared alike. But day after day, Woo-Ping bathed with the only soap in the camp. He was the only one who ate chicken dinners each evening and drank fresh coffee every morning while everyone else lived on rice. Woo-Ping was also the only one who smoked tailor-made cigarettes while everyone else smoked homemade cigarettes. He did not practice what he preached.

It was while we were in Woo-Ping's swampland camp that we learned something about the organization of the Communist guerrilla movement in Malaya. In February 1945, the Communist Anti-Jap Army included around 25,000 men divided into seven Regiments scattered throughout Malaya, with the Eighth Regiment forming in the far northern part. By what the men in the camp were telling us, there were only enough weapons to arm about half of this volunteer army. Because the Anti-Jap Army lacked arms, many soldiers, after receiving their initial military training, returned to their towns and farms and remained on call.

The Central Military Committee assigned each Regiment a section of the country and concealed each Regimental Headquarters deep in the jungle, garrisoned by around 100 men under the command of five officers, all captains. But all captains were not equal in power by any means.

The Number One Captain was a political commissar who was the regimental delegate to the Central Military Committee at the Supreme Headquarters of the Communist Army. Although his work was political, the Number One Captain was the commander with absolute power over his Regiment. The Number One Captains were always loyal Communists who held commanding positions in the Communist Party during the beginnings of the Communist Party in Malaya before the war started.

The other officers were the Right Captain and the Left Captain who handled most of the military detail, a Quartermaster Officer responsible for the Regiment's supplies, and a Propaganda Officer whose job was to sell Communism to the Malay people living in their Regiment's area.

Supreme command over all the Regiments rested in a Central Military Committee at the Supreme Military Headquarters of the Communist Army. This Central Military Committee was divided into two staffs, military and political, and controlled both the Malayan

Communist Party and the Anti-Jap Army. We never knew much about this committee, but we knew the Number One Captains of the various Regiments were members. And we discovered that even the smallest outpost throughout Malaya could not make a move without full approval from the top, the select Communists who comprised this Central Military Committee.

Generalissimo of the entire organization was a mysterious, well-educated Indo-Chinese who spoke fluent Chinese, French, and Russian. He had been a leader of the Malayan Communist Party since its inception around 1925. We heard him referred to as Li Tek and then another time as Li Teo, but those names did not mean much because he changed his name every week to avert recognition.

We learned that only full-fledged members of the Communist Party could become officers in the Anti-Jap Army. Soldiers were not always Communist Party members, but Party members held more responsible positions and received much better clothes and weapons.

Saltz and I had been at Woo-Ping's Third Regiment middle post several days when Duffy caught up with us on February 24th. As Duffy came limping into camp, two Chinese guerrillas had to hold him up and then carried him the final few yards to our basha. Duffy looked more dead than alive. With his swollen legs and feet from beriberi, he couldn't walk. He was also shaking from the fever that had just come back. It was both incredible and a relief to see that Duffy had made the trek, and Saltzman and I were more than thrilled to see him.

But although he was sick and frail, as soon as he sat down, he began yelling at me as loud as his weak condition would allow. "You son of a bitch! You bastards left us to save your butts!"

"Duff, we had to go," I said. "They ordered us to move on to arrange our escape from Malaya. We didn't know the orders we received would only mean moving to this camp."

"Ordered, Hump? Are you taking orders from the Communists and leaving your men to die?" Duffy barked back.

"You're out of line, Duff. We sent the medicine, and we couldn't do anything more for the two of you."

"Hump, Hansman's dead. Is that the best you can offer? You must live with this for the rest of your life and ask yourself, 'Could I have saved him?'"

"Yes, I will have to live with it," I answered.

We left it at that and discussed the matter later after Duffy rested and settled down.

Duffy told us what happened. "When we received the letter on February 12th, it was a terrible blow for both of us. I was furious about being left behind. Both Hansman and I took a turn for the worse. Hansman's fever was so high he couldn't read the note. Worse, the quinine water mentioned in the letter was missing from the bundle when the guide arrived. Only the cholera mix came in the package, no quinine water. The entry I put in my diary that day tells the story. 'February 12. Hell!'"

Duffy went on. "Here is the next day's entry. I will read it to you. 'February 13. About noon, I feel a little better today, but we almost lost Hansman this morning. I told the guerrillas to force the cholera mix down his throat. Although we are lying side by side on this darned wooden bench, I did not have the strength to do it. After the first two doses, he vomited, but the third one went down and stayed. He has been raving all day, and I am praying for him now. I feel he is working up to a deadly climax.'"

After he finished reading us the diary entry, Duffy looked up and said, "He was."

Duffy continued. "The next day, Hansman died with jungle fever. All that night of February 13, he breathed with a rasping noise in his throat. I have never heard death before, but maybe that was it. All night long, I forced the guerrillas to put wet rags on him, trying to break his fever, but it kept mounting. Then just about dawn, at 5:35, he stopped gasping. I crawled over closer to him, so weak from my fever that I almost fainted. I could not feel any heart action, so I grabbed his wrist. There was just a shadow of a pulse, frail and slow, and then he faded away."

I saw tears running down Duffy's face as he continued with his story about Hansman's passing.

"The next hours were worse than any nightmare because they were real," Duffy went on. "I lay there beside Hansman's body, hoping I was dreaming all this but knowing all the time it was true. I just laid there and stared at his body. Here was my friend, the fellow I had trained with back in the United States and traveled overseas with to fight the Japs. We ended up together in this God-forsaken jungle. And now he was gone.

"At about 10:00 a.m., the Chinese came for him. As I watched, they took off his shoes, wristwatch, and identification tags and handed them to me. They tied the body to a rattan mat. I made them put one dog tag back around his neck. They wanted to strip him, but I would not let them. That was the last I saw of him. I think they buried him in a shallow grave a mile or so away in the jungle. I never saw the grave."

Duffy paused and then continued telling us what happened after Hansman's death. "From then on, I improved. By February 19th, I felt I could travel. We received news through the grapevine about your current location, and although still weak, I was afraid to wait any longer. With two guerrilla guides armed with rifles, I left camp and headed in your direction to join you. My legs were weak, but we still made excellent progress on the first day. On the second day, as we sneaked across a highway, the guerrilla guide walking behind me grabbed me by the neck and threw me down into the tall grass. I landed on my face, and it almost knocked me out. An instant later, a truck loaded with Japanese troops raced by. I banged up my face a bit and got a bloody nose, but we went undetected by the Japs. On the fifth night, while crossing a road, another escape was even more narrow than the first. I was climbing out of the roadside ditch when a Chinese behind me grabbed my legs and dragged me back into the tall grass. He saved my life because a big car with two Japanese officers sitting in the back seat drifted past us at about 10 miles per hour. I held my breath as we hid just below the road out of sight in the grass-filled ditch. The next day it was difficult to walk because of these swollen legs. With the help of the two guides, I made the last long walk and arrived here at this outpost."

For the next two weeks after Duffy joined us, Saltzman and I looked after his needs the best we could and tried to nurse him back to health and into good enough condition to travel. We hoped to be moving again soon to the next destination we thought would be Supreme Headquarters.

Our goals were to stay alive, avoid the Japs, find Supreme Headquarters and a radio transmitter, and escape Malaya as fast as possible. Finding a radio to contact the Allies for help was crucial, and we thought for sure the Supreme Military Headquarters of the Communist Anti-Army would have one. We needed to find the Supreme Headquarters and the radio.

We doped Duffy with some herbs English Tom gave us to help him sleep at night. During the day, we walked him around the clearing for exercise to regain strength in his legs. I also bargained with English Tom for some hard-to-get healthy food to feed Duff and help him get well.

Duff failed to respond, so we went to Woo-Ping and demanded Duffy see an Indian doctor we heard lived on a rubber estate only hours away. Woo-Ping grumbled and growled but consented.

It is never a straightforward path in or out of Woo-Ping's camp. Woo-Ping set up this camp, so we knew he would know the best and easiest route to the rubber plantation and the doctor's house. It amazed us when we asked and Woo-Ping agreed to guide Duffy, as only he could, to see the Indian doctor.

Duffy said they waited together with several other Chinese soldiers on the edge of the jungle until nightfall. When it became dark, they waded through the swampland for two hours to a location where Woo-Ping had several sampans tied up at the shore of the Tasek Bera. After a sampan ride to the other side, they came to a pathway that led to the plantation. Woo-Ping said there might be Japanese in the plantation area, and they needed to be alert. They walked with caution down several rows of rubber trees through the plantation until they reached another path leading up to the house. Woo-Ping led Duffy to the back of the doctor's home at about midnight. When he knocked on the door, the doctor opened the door and said, "Good evening. Please come in."

The doctor, Duffy said, was a good guy who spoke excellent English. After he examined Duffy, his diagnosis was that he suffered from hookworm, malaria, and beriberi.

The doctor's house was like a small hospital. There were Chinese, Malaysian, and Indian patients who kept roaming around everywhere from room to room. Duff said he kept his .45 in his hand the entire time he was there. He almost shot one guy who poked his head into his room and screamed at him. Duffy said the doctor told him not to worry and ignore the man because he was crazy. But the crazy man almost drove Duffy crazy because he kept doing the same thing every few minutes over and over for the next hour.

Duffy's doctor insisted that Duffy's party stay all night at the house so he could tend to Duffy, but Woo-Ping refused point blank. Then the doctor said he would gather all the ingredients to mix medicines made for Duffy's illnesses. He said to send a runner for the medications in five days. Before they left, the doctor gave Duffy a surprising present: four books in English. They were *The History of St. Matthew*, an unknown adventure story, a geography book of Asia, and collected excerpts from famous English diaries. The natives had torn out the first few chapters of each of the books to use the pages for cigarette paper. They were the only reading materials available to us, so the missing pages did not concern us. The books were a kind gift that helped fill a void in our lives at Woo-Ping's camp.

We continued to help Duffy the best we could with no medications. After five days, we sent a runner back to the doctor's house to pick up the medicines the doctor said he would make for Duffy. The drugs did not arrive back until 10 days later, and the package did not contain mixed medications. There were six aspirin tablets, 20 powders of MacLean's medicine for Duffy's stomach disorder, and some quinine water for malaria and fever. Although not the mixed medications we wanted, they were better than no medication at all. Starting with the quinine water, we began Duffy on a rigorous course of treatment and rest. Duff, determined to get back on his feet, stuck with the schedule. If he did not adhere to the program, Duffy knew he would not survive.

As he took another giant slug of the quinine water, Duffy said, "I know I cannot hold us up, and I also know I can't survive alone among these Chinese guerrillas. I will do everything I can to regain my strength and get healthy enough to travel ASAP." Then he took another slug of the quinine water, laid down, and drifted off to sleep.

We all took it easy during this time and worked on nursing ourselves back to health. Besides Duffy's illnesses, Saltzman's burns were still trying to heal. I suffered from malnutrition and severe weight loss because I was living with the trots almost nonstop.

There were no Jap alerts because of our secluded location, so all day, Saltz and I did nothing but tend to Duffy, read, relax, and listen to the bug and animal sounds in the surrounding jungle. Our biggest concern now was the never-ending battle with mosquitoes. They were everywhere, and they were relentless.

It took a little while, but Duffy was over his anger at us for leaving him and Hansman behind. We discussed the matter more after he first arrived in camp, and I explained that we left them because we thought the letter we received said we were going to a headquarters where we could radio for help for us all. And we left it there.

Saltz and I told Duffy about the game of tag the Chinese invited us to play when we first arrived in camp and about a theatrical performance the guerrillas put on for us the second night at their social gathering.

"Duff, we were the guests of honor seated in the front row," I said. "The actors in the play were all guerrillas, plus Soo Ah, a Chinese girl from Singapore, who was a cabaret singer before joining the Communists."

"There is a woman in this camp who is a cabaret singer?" Duffy asked with amazement.

"Four women!" Saltz said. "They're as hard as the men in this

117

outfit. Soo Ah wears a grenade on her belt, and I think she can take care of herself pretty well."

Then I filled Duff in on how Saltz was trying to woo, one at a time, each of the few women in our camp. And so far, I might add, to my knowledge, without success. The pursuit of women was always a never-ending endeavor for Saltz wherever we were.

As Duff felt a little better, Saltz and I went off into the surrounding jungle for a few hours at a time to explore but never straying too far from camp. We found tiger tracks, traces of elephants, monkeys by the hundreds, and all kinds of trees and beautiful colored flowers. It was a sight to see.

All this time, Woo-Ping—the commanding officer of this guerrilla camp, a Third Regiment Anti-Jap Army middle post with more than 100 men—showed himself to be a 24-karat louse. This man was such a hypocrite. He preached about men being equal under Communism, but he never practiced it. In the weeks since he arrived, we watched him as he continued to feast on chicken and drink hot coffee in the shade of his basha while he marched his starving soldiers. Then one day, Woo-Ping gave an even better hypocritical exhibition of the old Party spirit.

The friendly Chinese we called English Tom did us a special favor by finding Duffy some good healthy food when he needed it. We wanted to reward him, so we gave him the fine-looking Swiss wristwatch that had belonged to Hansman. Woo-Ping was wearing the beautiful Swiss watch an hour later, and English Tom was wearing Woo Ping's old beat-up watch.

Not long after that, Woo-Ping went all out to show his true colors. Yung Han, the Junior commanding officer to Woo-Ping who earlier guided us through the jungle and became a friend of ours, was being transferred again to another post. Some Malay natives from around the area sent him a flag made by the natives' wives as a farewell gift. It was a regular Malayan Communist flag, blood-red with three golden stars. There were messages of appreciation from several of the natives written all over it, along with poems written for Yung Han's safety on his journey to his new post.

Yung Han was deeply touched as he accepted the gift from his friends, and he became emotional. At the sight of the flag and Yung Han's emotional response, Woo-Ping burst into loud laughter, walked over, grabbed the flag out of Yung Han's hands, and tossed it to one of the Chinese girls. He ordered her to make him a pair of socks. Yung Han was furious, and so were the other guerrillas who witnessed this hateful act. But no one dared breathe one breath of disapproval toward this influential Communist leader. There would be severe consequences if anyone did. He was a cold-hearted, cruel man, and everyone feared him.

On March 12th, two months and one day after we parachuted into the jungle and one month after arriving at Woo-Ping's Third Regiment middle post, a letter came for us. But again, we were disappointed. The letter was not from Supreme Headquarters. The message was from the Third Regiment Headquarters commander, Woo-Ping's superior commander. It directed us to proceed to his Third Regiment Headquarters.

I asked English Tom about the trek to the Third Regiment Headquarters.

He answered, "Many days south. You must cross the Muar River. Dangerous journey. Captain with more power than Woo-Ping at Third Regiment Headquarters."

There was nothing for us to do but obey because the friendship and direction of these Communist guerrillas were our only hope. Despite their reluctance to help us, they kept helping us, although not always the way we hoped.

CHAPTER 9

Third Regiment Headquarters

Four days later, Duff was strong enough to travel. On March 16th, after our month-long stay at this middle post, we started our trek to the Third Regiment Headquarters. Woo-Ping did not come out of his basha to say goodbye, and we did not go to Woo-Ping's basha to say goodbye. We despised the man because he was an arrogant, selfish, cruel dictator and not a respectable commander. For us, it was good riddance.

As we readied to leave, English Tom and many guerrillas from the Regiment clustered around our basha. They gave us some Japanese money and cigarettes as farewell gifts. All of us shouldered our equipment and lumbered off into the bush once again.

Woo-Ping assigned us a Chinese Communist guide named Chang and two Chinese guerrilla guards named Na Tom and Sung Fu, who carried rifles. Our trip would be one of the most grueling ordeals we had ever experienced.

Our lead guide, Chang, was a friendly, clean-cut, educated Chinese who spoke decent English. Na Tom was a very skinny Chinese with a large bucktooth, and he hated white men. We later named him Speedy because he always walked so fast. And Sung Fu, our bearer of equipment, was a filthy Chinese man who had a skin disease with ugly seeping sores.

It was now March 16th. The first day of this trek gave us an idea of what was in store for us for the next several days' journey to the Third Regiment Headquarters. First, we took two sampans across part of Tasek Bera. Then we walked for two hours in heavy rain through swampland with waist-high and sometimes neck-high water. We walked another four hours, slipping on the muddy trails through the thick jungle.

We reached a small two-basha Chinese outpost late that evening where we stayed for the night. After burning the leeches off each other, we tried to sleep, but the mosquitoes were buzzing in our ears. Their continued bites all night made it difficult to sleep. We later learned the Chinese established many small outposts like this one, scattered throughout the Malayan jungle. They used them for layovers for their runner communication system.

The second morning, Duff and I both woke up and could not see because of swollen eyes from mosquito and spider bites. The semi-cool water from a nearby stream helped enough with the swelling so we could see again. As we pushed on, Duff was holding up well, and for now, his fever had subsided. He could keep up a regular pace with the rest of us. For the next few days, the rain never stopped. We scraped our way through bamboo and waded through marshlands and mud. Leeches covered our bodies from head to toe at the end of each day.

On March 22nd, we reached another small outpost where a Malay native sold pigs. That night, Chang purchased the side of a pig and cooked us a wonderful hot Chinese meal. We spent the rest of the night and the following day resting. We needed a one-day rest period.

As we left the outpost, the same Malay native sold Chang a mouse deer for two dollars to take with us. We moved out, stocked with food for that night and maybe another day. The terrain changed. We started crossing through miles of grasslands. The guides said we needed to stay alert because big cats lived in the grasslands, and they would hide along the animal trails waiting for their prey. The rain kept coming day after day. If it stopped for a while, the mosquitoes would come out even worse than usual to devour us. That evening we stopped at another outpost where we ate our mouse deer for dinner and slept.

We left on March 24th in the pouring rain. We were now back in the thick jungle with all the now-familiar animal sounds. A horde of wild boars gave us a surprise that morning, but they were just as frightened as we were and took off running into the brush.

We waded through stream after stream, sometimes up to our waists for several hours as we approached the flooding Muar River. When we reached the riverbank, Chang told us to prepare to swim across the river. Then the two Chinese guards started arguing and boasting about who could swim better than the other. The Chinese were always bragging about who was the best or better at something or another. For example, they argued over who knew the best direction to take on our routes. One always needed to be better than the other.

After the guerrillas built a bamboo raft for the gear, we all started across the river. Duff was trying to keep everything on the bamboo raft while keeping his head above the six-foot deep water. Saltz almost lost one of his boots when it became stuck in the river bottom mud, but I grabbed it when it surfaced before it floated away downstream. Just as the water became neck deep, the two Chinese guerrillas screamed at the top of their lungs.

I said, "Chang! What are they screaming about?"

Chang answered, "They say, 'We are drowning, please save us!'"

So much for "excellent swimmers," I thought. So Saltzman grabbed the raft, and Duff and I helped the two boasting, now drowning Chinese to shore.

"You could have killed us all out there!" I yelled at the two Chinese. Then Saltz, Duff, and I all looked at each other and burst out laughing.

Chang said, "Chinese honor at stake. Never show you are not master, more honorable to die!"

"Well, they almost did just that," I said, shaking my head.

When crossing the streams and the Muar River, we again became covered with leeches. Still standing in thigh-high muddy water on the other side of the Muar, we could only help each other remove the leeches from the waist up. The others below the belt would have to wait until later.

I looked over at Duffy who was grasping onto the branch of a fern and said, "Duff, you okay?"

"Yeah, I'm okay. I am just tired, Hump. Real tired. My fever is back, and this swamp is tough going," Duff said as he let go of the fern and pushed forward. Duffy would soon need another good rest.

We came across a deserted compound and stayed there out of the rain, mud, swamp, and thick jungle for the night. Everything was too wet to build a fire, so we could not burn off all the leeches. The sores from the heads left under our skin became an issue for us all.

On March 25th, we left the compound late in the morning, covered with mosquito bites and still covered with the blood-sucking parasites not yet filled up with our blood enough to fall off on their own. Over the next few days, everything changed for the better. We traveled through territory covered with ferns, coconut trees, orchards, lime trees, banana trees, and lots of coffee beans. Duffy's fever broke, and he regained some strength. As soon as we could, we built a fire and spent more than an hour helping each other remove all the leeches. The leech bites covered our bodies head to toe with leech sores. We would need medical attention when we arrived at Third Regiment Headquarters. During the last days of our trip to the Third Regiment, there was plenty of nutritious food. The healthy food helped restore our malnourished bodies.

On March 30th, we reached another small Chinese outpost located not too far from the Third Regiment Headquarters. The rain stopped, so we built a fire and enjoyed some hot Chinese tea and hot cooked rice. We sat around the fire, relaxed, and talked with Chang for a while. Chang asked a lot of questions about the United States and our government. He also told us a bit about himself. He said his family owned a 10-acre rubber estate before the Japanese occupation in December 1941. When the Japanese came through the Kuala Lumpur area during their southern invasion of the Malay Peninsula in 1942, they confiscated the estate. When the Japanese came through, he said there were two choices: either become a Japanese soldier or die. Chang told us he acted like he was a loyal Japanese soldier in order to live. But one night, when the camp guards fell asleep, he slipped away into the jungle. While he was hiding out with some Chinese, he joined the Communist guerrillas.

After our long talk with Chang, we were all looking for a place to settle down for a good night's sleep. We soon realized, for some unknown reason, that this outpost housed quite a few women. We found them everywhere, spread all over the camp sleeping in all kinds of different places. Saltz thought he had died and gone to heaven as he walked around looking for a place to sleep and saw all the women.

Later that evening, we think Saltz found the Malayan companionship he had been searching for since the day we parachuted from the *Postville Express*.

The next morning, Saltz had a big smile on his face and Chang, Speedy, and Sung Fu had already left to go back to Woo-Ping's camp. It seemed we were in a Chinese-run, Pony Express–like, underground operation that took us from post to post. Talib was the first leg, then George and Georgette, and now Chang finished his portion of the responsibility.

After being reenergized with some nutritious food and a good night's sleep, we left for the Third Regiment Headquarters with two new armed guides assigned to us from this outpost. With more waist-high water streams to cross and still having to go up and down many steep hills, we pushed on for two-and-a-half hours straight without rest that morning. After 15 days of hell, we arrived at Third Regiment Headquarters on what turned out to be a befitting day, April 1st, April Fools' Day.

We dreamed big dreams about these headquarters, picturing an expansive U.S. Army–like camp resembling Fort Sheridan back in Chicago. We imagined a radio room equipped with a radio transmitter to arrange our escape from the Malayan jungle. Instead, we were fooled again. It was like every other guerrilla camp we had encountered, a clearing about 200 yards across surrounded by the Malayan jungle with old beat-up bashas and the air thick with mosquitoes everywhere we went. The guides led us through the clouds of mosquitoes to an open-air basha where we would sleep that night.

The next morning, after almost no sleep and our eyes swollen shut from mosquito and spider bites, none of us could see. We asked one of our guides to lead us down to the nearby stream to refresh ourselves and put water on our eyes. After dunking our faces in the semi-cool water, the swelling subsided, and we could open our eyes again. Our Pointie Talkie book did not have the word mosquitoes, so we had a tough time conveying to the Chinese our need for a remedy to have some relief from the mosquito bites during the night. The mosquitoes did not seem to bother the Chinese, but they were eating us alive. After another lousy night of mosquito bites and a morning of dunking our heads in the stream for relief, the Chinese realized we needed defense from our mosquito enemies when we slept at night.

Later that day, one of our Chinese guides came to our basha with two blankets and a piece of heavy woven rug for us as cover-up defenses against the mosquitoes. He gave Duffy and Saltzman the blankets, and I received the small part of a rug. The six-foot-long patchwork blankets were old and musty and not very thick. My piece of the woven rug was thick and measured only about two-and-a-half feet wide and five feet long. The blankets were satisfactory for Saltz and Duffy, but the rug was hot because it was so thick. And since we were near the equator, it never cooled off at night unless it poured down rain.

There was also another problem. I am six feet two inches tall with a five-foot rug for a cover-up. There was always a decision to make, whether to cover my head or my feet. If I covered my head and face, the mosquitoes bit my ankles all night, and besides that, it was sweltering hot and suffocating. If I covered my feet and ankles, they bit my head and face. I shuffled back and forth with my rug in my never-winning battle against the mosquito pests all night long.

They say rank has its privileges, but if that was why they gave me the rug and not one of the musty blankets, it was a terrible mistake. But we had no choice. From then on, we slept under the rug and blankets. It was better than no protection at all.

In this Third Regiment Headquarters, we met an 18-year-old Chinese named Wong Tek Swan. He looked mature for his age. He had a round face, and when he smiled, it was like a giant ray of sunshine.

Tek Swan walked up to us and said in perfect English, "Good Morning, Americans. It is a pleasure to meet you."

Saltzman asked, "How is it you speak such perfect English without an accent?"

Tek Swan smiled his gracious, warm smile and answered Saltzman, "From American movies. When I grew up in Singapore, going to the movies was almost free for students. I went to the movies every Saturday and Sunday. I know America very well from these movies. I went to a movie theater on Saturday morning and stayed until the afternoon. Then I went back again that night. Some days I would watch four or five American movies in a row. I learned the American language very well that way."

Tek Swan liked and respected us right away because we were Americans. And as we came to know him better, we developed a mutual respect. He became a lifesaver because he was the official interpreter for the Chinese Communist high-ranking officers at this Third Regiment Headquarters. He later told us that he only translated what he knew the big shots wanted to hear during one of our communications with the Chinese.

"I couldn't tell them everything you said because they wouldn't like it, and then they wouldn't like you," Tek Swan said.

He was a gem. He told us the Communist Party brought him into the jungle to write their Communist propaganda and teach in the school. No one else ever taught these local natives how to read or write, so the Communists were making the most of this opportunity. They wrote all the teaching manuals and school pamphlets with a Communist slant. They taught from Karl Marx and rewrote the Russian training manuals in Chinese. Each day's teaching session started with the Russian "International" song, and each day ended with it. The Communist indoctrination occurred in every facet of Malay life, and the Communist Party's recruitment continued day after day.

As we roamed around that day, another Chinese with apparent Mongoloid features walked up to meet us. He wore an Australian Army officer's shirt and trousers, Australian boots and leggings, and a Japanese officer's cap with a dried bloodstain on the right side. He greeted us in English and told us his name was Ko Shin. He said he was an officer in Chiang Kai-shek's Chinese Army in China but now was with the Communist Party in Malaya. How he ended up here among the Communists in Malaya he did not disclose.

Ko Shin said his job was a drillmaster, and he was here to instruct all the Third Regiment outpost officers that came to Headquarters for training. He surprised us because when he said the Japanese occupied a town called Segamat located 30 miles due east of us, he disclosed where the Anti-Jap Army hid this Regiment Headquarters in the jungle. None of the Communist guerrillas we met before Ko Shin ever told us the name of a nearby city that would reveal our exact location. In prior camps, although we always seemed to find out, the Anti-Jap Army kept the precise areas of the various posts secret. Maybe it was because they thought if we ever escaped Malaya alive, which was now questionable, we might tell the British the locations of the Communist Regiment outposts. Or if the Japanese captured us, we might disclose the sites to them. It was becoming clear that the Chinese Communists intended to fight the Japanese and later the British to control Malaya.

With this additional information, Duffy pulled out his map of Malaya and said, "Looks like we are 75 miles due east of where we bailed out. With the routes we took to arrive here, it looks like over the past 82 days since landing in Malaya, we have traveled close to 130 miles through the jungle."

I said, "Thanks for that info, Duff. That is a long haul. Maybe with a little help we can be out of this jungle soon."

Then I asked Ko Shin, "Any news about any other American Airmen? I am missing six members of my crew."

Ko Shin answered, "I have heard no news of other Airmen."

Ko Shin said there are two high-ranking Captains at this Third Regiment Headquarters. Their names were Woo Ko Chung and Ah Sing, and I would meet them later that night.

Many Chinese, somewhat better dressed than those we lived with before, lounged in the clearing, smoking and talking. We learned these were the Captains and other Regimental Officers who were there for Ko Chin's training.

Later that day, Tek Swan came to me and said, "Many of the Regimental commanders have gathered here for training, and they would like to talk with you. We will soon go to the commander's house where you will meet the Regimental Captains of the Third Regiment Headquarters and talk with all the visiting Regimental outpost commanders. They want to talk about America and Communism."

After the evening meal, Tek Swan came to lead us to the commander's basha. It did not differ from any other basha except it was longer with fresh bamboo flooring for each Captain to sleep on and had a new palm leaf roof. There were five or six well-dressed Chinese men in their 20s sitting on the bamboo floor. The Captain of the Third Regiment welcomed us, and Tek Swan did the interpreting.

"Hello, and welcome. My name is Woo Ko Chung. I am Number One Captain of the Third Regiment. To my right is Right Captain Ah Sing."

"Hello," I replied. "It is a pleasure to meet you. My name is Major Donald J. Humphrey, and to my right are First Lieutenant William Duffy and First Lieutenant Cliff Saltzman. Woo Ko Chung, we have written letters to Supreme Military Headquarters. Have they received any of our letters?"

Woo Ko Chung answered, "I do not know. Write another letter, and I will deliver it to the Supreme Military Committee next week."

"Okay, thank you. I will write another letter," I replied.

With that said, the five Chinese wanted to tell us about the five stages in man's development in a society, starting with the cave dweller up through Capitalism, Socialism, and then Communism. And Communism, in their opinion, was the ultimate form of government for all people.

One of the Chinese worth pointing out was an intellectual-looking type with wire-rimmed glasses who, they said, carried his cased violin with him everywhere he went. He walked two hours from a nearby outpost through the hot steamy jungle with this delicate violin in hand for this meeting. We did not hear him play, but he perhaps entertained the others after we left. He was the most determined to explain to us, along with the others, why Communism was so much better than Capitalism. They spent several hours using Wong Tek Swan as their interpreter, trying to persuade us to Communism.

As we debated, neither side's lecture ever swayed the other side's opinion, but they gave it their best to convince us how much better Communism was than Capitalism.

Later, in private, Tek Swan said, "I couldn't tell them what you said because it would have angered them too much."

And he was right to do so. We now lived in their country and their jungle camp. They fed us, and they protected us from the Japanese. The wise Tek Swan kept everything as copacetic as possible.

After we debated with the Chinese, I wrote another letter for Woo

Ko Chung to take to Supreme Headquarters. I explained we would need their help to assist us with our journey to Supreme Military Headquarters and that we needed to use their radio to contact the Allies to arrange our pickup location. In the letter, I promised that if they assisted us, the Americans would airdrop weapons and ammunition into Malaya to help the Chinese Communist Anti-Army fight the Japanese. When I finished, I gave the letter to Woo Ko Chung, and he left for Supreme Headquarters two days later.

During the long weeks while we remained in the Communist Anti-Jap Third Regiment Headquarters waiting for Woo Ko Chung to return, Ah Sing treated us with kindness. He ordered the women in the camp to mend our clothes, and we ate well. We rested as our leech sores were healing. Duff's fever subsided for the time being, but the mosquitoes were still an endless bother. While none of us were okay, the rest sure helped us feel better.

We became friendly with Tek Swan over the following days. He spoke excellent English and was a pleasure to have around. Saltzman noted that because of Tek Swan, we were realizing more and more the tremendous amount of ill will Britain had piled up for herself in this part of the world before Japan invaded Malaya in 1941.

Tek Swan was the first Chinese Communist who came right out in the open to express the view that the British would have to fight the Communist Army before they could again dominate the country of Malaya. He admitted that the primary aim of the Communist guerrilla movement was not only to fight the Japanese but to build up strength for the battle coming later against the British.

Unlike many less intelligent guerrillas, Tek Swan was not lulled into a false sense of security by the growing strength of the Communist forces. He expected a fight with the British. He hoped the Communist guerrillas would continue to work day and night to gain more and more strength so they would be ready for the battle when it came. From other guerrillas, we learned that Tek Swan was the Chief Protégé of the Third Regiment commander, Woo Ko Chung, who was grooming him to be one of the future Malayan Communist leaders.

On May 4th, Woo Ko Chung returned to camp from his trip to the Central Military Committee at the Headquarters of the Supreme Commander of the Communist Party and the Anti-Jap Army. He called us to his basha. We knew something was up because the English-speaking Chinese in the camp had been coming up to us all day saying goodbye and telling us we would soon go to America. Our minds were racing. We thought maybe we were going home.

Upon entering his basha, we could see Woo Ko Chung was pleased. He was excited. And when a Chinese is excited, you can bet your boots something significant is in the fire. After a preliminary ceremonial cup of coffee, he told us, with Tek Swan interpreting, that we would soon be back in America. Then, with a smile on his face, he handed me a folded letter and said the letter explained everything.

I took the folded letter from Woo Ko Chung and unfolded it. I opened the letter dated January 20th and addressed to "The B-29 airmen shot down on January 11, 1945." The date of the letter was just nine days after the *Postville Express* went down. We looked at each other and hoped for good news. With much anticipation, I opened the letter. It read:

Dear fellow countrymen:

On the 11th of January, I had the thrill of seeing six B-29s fly over my headquarters. I said at the time that if any of you ever had the misfortune of crashing in this place that you would crash near me. But last night I got the bad news that you did crash-land and over 100 miles away at that. If this letter reaches you as I hope it will, it will introduce to you men from the 6th guerrilla Regiment. These men will bring you to me. I've already radioed SEAC (Southeast Asia Command) of the efforts to rescue you. So, with luck, we should get you out in about six weeks. During your stay here it will be my great pleasure to be your guest. I say guest because I have not seen or talked to an American for many weeks. So when you get here I will throw a big feast for you and believe it or not there will be wine. I am enclosing a frat card, as an assurance to you that everything is OK. In about two weeks I'll come and meet you halfway and bring you here myself. At the present it is impossible to come. As you can well imagine I'd like to shoot the bull with you, but that will have to wait until we get together over a bottle of wine. For security reasons I have cut my name from the frat cards, and I am using a cover name so don't be alarmed.

(Signed) J. Jack Bussy,
Commanding Officer,
Allied Detachment, U.S. Army

We did not know what to think. Each of us read the letter under the flickering light of the oil lamp. We were all having the same doubts about it because of the odd wording, the faulty construction of the sentences, and the use of the word *frat*, which fraternity men hate. And there were not any men from the Sixth Guerrilla Regiment with the letter.

We asked Woo Ko Chung what he thought about the last point. He said the letter came from the Supreme Military Committee of the Communist Party. We then explained our skepticism and our suspicion that the Japanese might have planted the message. He seemed disappointed to hear we doubted the letter's authenticity since it came from the Supreme Military Headquarters.

Then he said, with Tek Swan translating, "There should be little danger on the passage from this camp to the Sixth Regiment Headquarters. If you want to go, I will write you the letters of protection you will need when you leave my Third Regiment jurisdiction and enter the Sixth Regiment's jurisdiction. I will also provide you with a guide and an escort of eight soldiers with rifles and Tommy Guns from my Third Regiment Anti-Jap Army."

Then he warned us that we might pass up a chance to get out of Malaya if we did not take the risk and go.

That decided it for us. If there was even an off chance this Bussy guy was an American and not a Jap trying to trap us, then we should take it.

I asked Ko Shin, "How far to the American and the Sixth Regiment Headquarters?"

Ko Shin said, "Long journey, 200 miles north to Sixth Regiment."

Later that day, a runner came with news saying Woo-Ping had been battling a Japanese patrol at the rubber plantation near his Regiment. Since we needed to pass through Woo-Ping's Third Regiment middle post, we waited until we received word that the area was all clear before heading north to the Sixth Regiment to find J. Jack Bussy and a radio.

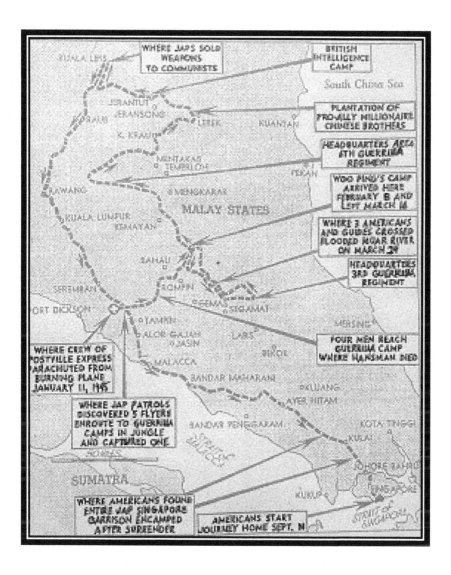

WHERE JAPS SOLD WEAPONS TO COMMUNISTS

BRITISH INTELLIGENCE CAMP

South China Sea

PLANTATION OF PRO-ALLY MILLIONAIRE CHINESE BROTHERS

HEADQUARTERS AREA 6TH GUERRILLA REGIMENT

WOO PING'S CAMP ARRIVED HERE FEBRUARY 8 AND LEFT MARCH 14

WHERE 3 AMERICANS AND GUIDES CROSSED FLOODED MOAR RIVER ON MARCH 29

HEADQUARTERS 3RD GUERRILLA REGIMENT

FOUR MEN REACH GUERRILLA CAMP WHERE HANSMAN DIED

WHERE CREW OF OSTVILLE EXPRESS PARACHUTED FROM BURNING PLANE JANUARY 11, 1945

WHERE JAP PATROLS DISCOVERED 5 FLYERS ENROUTE TO GUERRILLA CAMPS IN JUNGLE AND CAPTURED ONE

WHERE AMERICANS FOUND ENTIRE JAP SINGAPORE GARRISON ENCAMPED AFTER SURRENDER

AMERICANS START JOURNEY HOME SEPT. 11

MALAY STATES

SUMATRA

CHAPTER 10

200-Mile Trek

Three days later, on May 7, 1945, 37 days after we arrived on April 1st, we left Third Regiment Headquarters. By the grace of God, we had survived in the Japanese-occupied Malayan jungle since the day we parachuted out of the *Postville Express* 117 days ago on January 11th. Now, Saltzman, Duffy, and I were headed north to the Sixth Regiment Headquarters of the Communist Anti-Jap Army to find Commander J. Jack Bussy.

With eight guards packed with rifles and Tommy Guns and our letters of protection, we hit the trail. The trip from the Third Regiment

Headquarters to the Sixth Regiment Headquarters was more than 200 miles, and it was going to take three weeks. We expected to cross many streams, lakes, swamps, and rivers, including the dreaded Tasek Bera swampland lake. We knew it would be a long trek, and we knew it would not be easy.

The trek, challenging enough, became worse because almost as soon as we were on the trail, Duffy became ill with fever on day three and stayed sick most of the trip. I had another bout of diarrhea, and we feared that Saltz was now also infected with malaria. Duffy staggered along, trying hard to keep up. Every time we looked back at him, he waved and motioned us to keep moving. There was nothing we could do for him. I kept thinking he would end up like Hansman in an unmarked jungle grave if we could not find a radio soon and escape Malaya. Duffy needed a hospital ASAP.

Since our trip to the Third Regiment Headquarters more than a month ago, the floodwaters had receded. That made crossing the streams and rivers much more manageable and the jungle paths much less muddy. It also seemed like these guides were taking us on a less challenging route back through the jungle.

One night we thought a herd of elephants would trample our camp. First, we heard loud elephant calls. Their calls became louder and louder. Then we could hear the elephants crashing and ripping through the trees, and the sounds were getting closer and closer to our makeshift bashas. It sounded like they were coming right for us. We knew everything would be fine when we saw the Chinese laughing at our concern.

Nine days of rough hiking through the jungle, fighting mosquitoes night and day, brought us back to the shores of Tasek Bera on May 16th. After an hour tromping through swampland water up to our waists, we came to some sampans tied to a tree. I again found it very difficult to board since they did not build the sampans for people as tall as I was.

We were back in Tasek Bera, the swampland lake with moss-filled trees and low-hanging branches filled with snakes, spiders, and all kinds of birds. The swamp water in this area had such a foul odor that it was challenging to breathe. We knew Tasek Bera was the home of freshwater crocodiles, but who knew what else roamed through those murky waters? We zigzagged through the trees and swamp brush for two hours. With cramped and numb legs from sitting still so long, we reached the shore at Woo-Ping's camp on the other side.

We entered Woo-Ping's camp wet, tired, and hungry, and right away, English Tom greeted us with a big smile and gave us some glorious news in his broken English. "War over in Europe. Germany surrendered! Hitler dead!"

As tired as we were, we hugged each other and jumped around like young school kids on the last day of school. We screamed, "Victory! Victory for the Allies! The European war has ended in a victory for the Allies!"

Even though we were close to death, celebrating in a Chinese military camp in the middle of Japanese-occupied Malaya, I remember the wonderful feeling this good news gave us.

With Germany defeated over two weeks ago, we knew the full weight of the Allies would now swing against the Japanese, and our chances of leaving Malaya alive had risen to at least 50–50. Before departing from Woo-Ping's camp, we commemorated the Allied victory over Germany with our Chinese friends stationed at the middle post. English Tom, Bartholomew, and Yung Han who had returned joined us for a celebratory rice dinner. Duff, Saltz, and I drank a toast with rice wine to Hitler's death. After a pleasant dinner with our Chinese friends and with the added enthusiasm because of the good news, we left that night to continue our journey.

Woo-Ping assigned us a new Chinese lead guide who could speak a little English and another armed guerrilla who would be our cook. Woo-Ping located his middle post campsite on a peninsula formed by the jagged Tasek Bera channels. The location kept the Regiment's middle post garrison safe from the Japanese but made it difficult to travel to and from the camp. We crossed one of the water inlets when we came into Woo-Ping's middle post camp, and now we were going to pass through a broader, more treacherous channel going out.

Our first night's journey from Woo-Ping's camp on our way to find Bussy was one of the most dangerous and scariest nights of our entire time in the jungle. It was not a fear of the Japs; it was the fear of crossing the Tasek Bera again. The two Chinese guides warned us that the path they chose on this side of Woo-Ping's camp would be a lot more challenging than the route we had just crossed.

It was a horrible undertaking that night. Our guide said we were first going to wade through the swamp to reach the shore to cross the Tasek Bera. We struggled for three hours through a swampland like the Florida Everglades with water sometimes up to our chests. Knowing that freshwater crocodiles and who knows what other creatures surrounded us did not ease our minds. We again saw snakes hanging in tree limbs, and the mysterious unknown rustling in the darkness added to our fears. We did not know which swampland creature would get us first. It was a scary three hours.

We reached some semi-dry ground and trudged through the mud for another hour to the edge of the lake. There we found two dugouts tied to a tree. We left the other guerrillas behind at Woo-Ping's, so there were five of us now—the three of us and two guerrilla guides. We squeezed into two small dugouts built for four. With all the weight, it left only an inch of freeboard on each side. On the lead dugout's front end, one torch provided the only light to guide us through the thick maze of trees and hanging tree limbs in the night's darkness.

We needed to sit still in the handmade canoes for fear of capsizing them. If we went to sleep during the night and leaned sideways, the bodyguards poked us in the back and gave us hell. At last, just about dawn, we reached one of the other shores of the large Tasek Bera inlet and ended up almost across from Woo-Ping's camp. It seemed like we had made little progress after spending all night on the swampland lake, but we were thankful to have the horrors of Tasek Bera behind us.

Battered and exhausted from crossing the Tasek Bera, we were surprised when a new Sakai tribe met us on the shore. They were just as friendly as our prior Sakai friends. They guided us through some paths, up the hill from the shore, and into a clearing.

The Sakai looked like the Sakai that Saltzman and I lived with before, but we could tell they were a different tribe because the 20 huts in this village were on stilts. Our prior Sakai friends constructed their huts on top of the cut-off tree trunks.

Fifty village natives clad only in loincloths stood staring at us with wide eyes. Like the Sakai we met earlier, these Sakai natives had never seen an American or a white person before. The Sakai, with smiles ear to ear, examined us from head to toe. They measured their body parts against ours, laughing and giggling whenever we talked. The Sakai, fascinated with me because of my six-foot-two-inch height, watched my every move.

We found ourselves surrounded by bare-breasted Sakai women wearing only tiny loincloths. One shapely, well-endowed, beautiful teenage girl dashed up to Saltz and gave him a pineapple. Saltz turned my direction with a big smile and asked, "Is this heaven?"

An older man presented us with a goat as a welcoming present. They later slaughtered it and cooked it for our evening meal. They showed us to one of their huts built on stilts and motioned us to go up a rattan rope ladder into what would be our home for a while.

We lived with this Sakai tribe for several days because Duffy's malaria and fever were back, worse than before. I had been suffering from a lousy case of diarrhea for the past two weeks and was very weak. Saltzman was still battling malaria. We all needed some time to heal, and the Sakai took good care of us. We ate very well while we were with them. They provided us with all kinds of jungle fruits, roots, and meat from various animals. The Sakai were a godsend. I do not think we would have survived without them.

These Sakai tribe members were about four feet to four feet six inches tall and muscular with powerful arms and legs. The women took care of the babies, and the men hunted for food. They went by a strict social order. The head man was in command, and he made that clear to everyone.

All the men and women had cigarettes hanging from their lips almost all the time, even when they were busy doing a chore. The Sakai were enchanting and loving people, which was ironic since their ancestors were headhunters.

The next day, several Sakai men woke us up early to follow them out of the village into the jungle. They wanted to show us how they dug enormous pits in the trails and covered them with brush and leaves to trap the giant Asian elephants and other animals. They also showed us where and how they set different traps and snares all along the animal trails.

Their hunting skills were incredible. The Sakai men were short but very athletic and could run fast while hurling their handmade spears at animals. When we came across a herd of wild boars that day, two Sakai men chased one of them and speared it while running full speed. It was intriguing and impressive to watch them at work.

They also showed us which nuts and roots were good to eat and where to find bananas, papaya, pineapple, and durian. When we went on a hunting trip with the Sakai, we never went home empty-handed, and they always seemed to have plenty of food on hand to eat.

Another day, while Duffy continued to rest and the Sakai women fed him good nourishing food to regain his strength, some men took Saltz and me hunting again. Like the other Sakai who took us hunting before, the men here used 8- to 10-foot bamboo blowguns along with their spears.

They hollowed out, cleaned, and polished the interior of the bamboo poles until their blowguns were ready to use. Next, they took a dart from a line of darts tied to their rattan belt. They dipped the sharp end into a pouch, also on their belt, containing curare, a poison mixture. The dart was small, only about two inches long with a puff of feathers on the tail end. After dipping the dart into the curare, they inserted it into the bottom end of the blowgun. Their game that day was the monkeys perched high in the trees, studying our every move. A Sakai aimed the blowgun at one monkey. With one massive puff into the lower end of the blowgun, he shot the dart through the air into the monkey sitting high in the tree. When the dart hit, the monkey jumped and tried to pull the dart out of its skin. Two seconds later, the monkey began shaking and then fell out of the tree to the ground, dead. They rushed over to the monkey and tied its hands and feet together with rattan vines found nearby growing in the jungle.

One problem with eating the monkey meat was that they looked like small children after skinning and cleaning them. It was suitable meat to eat, but it had a wild, bitter taste. Mouse deer was better. It was like venison, but we seldom ate mouse deer outside a Sakai camp. On the hunting trips, we watched them shoot all kinds of animals with their blowguns. We saw them kill wild boar, mouse deer, raccoon, possum, and even snakes. It was fascinating to watch them hunt.

On May 23rd, after six or seven days with this Sakai tribe, our leading Chinese guide decided Duffy was strong enough and urged us to go on. We left early the next morning and walked on animal trails through a more tropical jungle. We walked until dusk the first day and then stopped to make camp. While the guides completed the lean-to bashas for us for the night, we found a crisp, clean jungle stream nearby to bathe in while monkeys watched us from above.

We kept walking the jungle animal trails from dawn to dark every day. But toward the end of the fourth day, on May 27th, Duffy's fever came back. He was too weak to go any farther. We stopped early that day to give him a rest. The guides built a basha large enough for the three of us with a floor made of fresh-cut bamboo tied together and a palm leaf roof. We ate some cold rice, and then we all fell asleep.

At midnight, Duffy woke up with a high fever and went running like a maniac into the jungle. Saltz and I jumped up and ran after him. We caught him and, after a struggle, brought him back to the basha. After a few minutes, Duffy laid down and passed out. When he was out, we bound his hands and feet to the bamboo bed with rattan to keep him from running into the jungle again. Duffy slept the rest of the night. In the morning, his fever broke, and he shivered and shook all over. He shook so hard the whole basha trembled.

Saltz and I went down to where the guides were cooking rice and hot tea. We tried to tell our Chinese guide that Duffy was so sick he could not walk. The Chinese guides came up to look at Duffy and let us know we needed to keep moving because we were deep in the jungle with several more days to walk and only enough rice for a few more days. We told them we needed some more quinine water for Duffy. One guide went to his pack and returned with the green bottle filled with quinine water. But when Saltz and I propped Duff up to have him drink the quinine water, he could not keep it down. Duffy's inability to keep down the quinine water upset the head guide, and he let us know again that we must go on and leave Duffy in the jungle. Duffy's human life and suffering, from the Chinese guerrillas' way of looking at things, did not matter. Their culture differed from ours.

Our head guide spoke some English but only a few words. From my sack of meager belongings, I took out the Pointie Talkie book that came with our jungle survival kit attached to our parachutes. Saltz and I searched through the book and found the right question: "Where is a doctor?" On the opposite page was the same question in Chinese. We showed the Chinese the question, but we could not find an answer in the book that satisfied them. So they turned around and went back down to their basha near the stream.

Saltz and I talked over our situation and decided they would not leave us there, but there was still the problem of not having enough food unless we could get Duffy well enough to get back on the trail. We tried several times to prop him up and pour quinine water down his throat. It always came back up. We laid him back down and retied him to the bamboo in case the fever returned and he tried to run into the jungle again.

About noon, the head guide came back to our basha. He wanted to see the Pointie Talkie book again. I gave him the book, and he thumbed through it until he found the word *doctor* on the Chinese page. We looked at the English side and found that he was talking to us about a doctor. He made walking motions by moving his arms back and forth and stepping up and down in place while pointing to the word *doctor* in the book. He said, "I go, I go." He was telling us he would walk to get a doctor. Wonderful! Now someone would find a doctor for Duff who was still out cold next to us in the basha.

When the Chinese guide thought he had successfully demonstrated his intention to leave and bring back a doctor, he went back down to the guides' basha. After our discussion, we felt one of them would soon leave to find help, but nobody was moving. About an hour later, the head guide walked off into the jungle.

At dusk, Duffy was still sleeping, so Saltzman and I went down to the stream, took a bath, and ate some hot cooked rice and jungle spinach with our cooking guide. Before dark, we went back to our basha, checked on Duffy, laid down, and went to sleep.

We woke up at dawn, and Duffy was still out cold. We sat him up, but he would not drink the quinine water and passed out again. His fever had subsided for now, and he didn't seem chilled. So Saltz and I went down to have breakfast with the cooking guide and ate the usual hot cooked rice and drank hot tea while we waited.

Since we were short on rice, we did not eat at noon. We laid around with Duff, hoping he would improve enough to wake up, drink some quinine water and keep it down. It was a quiet afternoon, but Duffy was too quiet, passed out cold. I was worried he would not make it out of Malaya if we did not find help soon.

"How did we get into this mess, Hump?" Saltz asked.

"God willing, Saltz, we will be out of this mess soon so we can find Duffy a hospital."

That afternoon, a short, stocky Chinese man wearing only a loincloth and no shirt or shoes came walking out of the jungle with our head guide. Our cook guide joined them at the edge of the water. After conversing for several minutes, the head guide and the stranger came walking up to our basha. Our new guest motioned to Saltzman and me to prop up Duffy.

We untied Duffy and sat him up. The unknown visitor lifted Duffy's head, looked him over, and then laid him back down. He turned to Saltzman and me, bowed, turned on his heel, and walked off into the jungle. The head guide told us by using the Pointie Talkie book that the man was a doctor. With more searching and pointing and hand gesturing, we understood that he was an inside doctor and would return soon.

The Chinese and Malay natives saw inside doctors for inside disorders and outside doctors for outside disorders. Duffy was suffering from an inside disease, so he needed an inside doctor.

Late in the afternoon the next day, we heard some loud yelling from the jungle on the other side of the stream. Saltz and I jumped up at the sound of this loud yelling and ran down to join the guides who were now yelling back in Chinese to someone on the other side of the stream. We could not understand their words, but somebody coming through the jungle was screaming for help. The two guides started running across the stream through the knee-high water toward the screams on the other side.

Saltz and I stopped when we saw the short, Chinese inside doctor coming out of the jungle. Still dressed in only a loincloth, he came straight toward us with both hands grasped to a short piece of rattan wrapped around the head of a giant python. Straddling the colossal python, he dragged it across the shallow stream. When the python's tail hit the water, it seemed to wake up and whipped around back and forth. The small-framed doctor had a terrible time keeping it under control, even with the rattan pulled around its neck. Both guides ran toward him and grabbed the python to help, but the snake was so huge that it flipped all three of them around. When everyone could maintain a good hold on it, they struggled but brought the python through the stream onto the bank. They stretched it out to full length on the ground close to the cook's basha. It was about 20 feet long and 12 inches around. I will never know how the inside doctor captured the giant snake alone and brought it as far as he did.

Our Chinese guide who always cooked for us ran forward, jumping with glee with a large knife in hand. Our excited cook was about to dissect the snake when the inside doctor stepped forward, held up his hand, and said something in Chinese. The cook-guide then stepped back while everyone else held this tremendous snake down on the stream bank. I do not know what the inside doctor said to the guide because it was in Chinese, but it was something to this effect: "Keep your damn hands off my python!"

With an eight-inch knife that had been tied to his belt, the inside doctor started cutting open the snake just behind its head and then made a long slit down its belly. After he cut a three-foot opening, he reached into the snake's belly and pulled out a smaller snake about five feet long. He bowed to our cook and handed him the smaller snake. The smaller snake delighted our cook, but he still had his eye on the giant python.

The inside doctor continued to slice the belly of the python wide open down to its tail. Then he reached inside to cut out some red-colored glands, the python's choice parts that he wanted. Next, he took a tin cup tied to his rattan belt and dropped his python's select cuts into it. Then he stood up, bowed to the cook, and presented the python to him in a grand sweeping gesture with his hand. With the other guide's help, the cook jumped in and cleaned the giant snake and prepared to cook it for dinner.

The inside doctor took his tin cup and walked toward the stream. I followed behind him to watch his procedure. He stooped down to wash the python parts in the stream and then dropped them back into the cup. He looked up at me, bending his tin cup in all different shapes before he pressed it back to round again. I think he was showing me the cup was pure tin. There were many tin mines in Malaya. Because of the war, they did not have any alloys to mix with the pure tin to make it into a hard, firm cup.

Next, the inside doctor arranged some rocks in a circle, gathered some wood, and built a small fire on the bank inside a stone circle. He filled his pure tin cup that contained the python parts with clean stream water to just over half full. Then he took several roots or herbs he had tied to his rattan belt, and with his knife, he scraped and cut them into slivers and washed them in the stream. Then, one by one, he cut them up into smaller pieces and dropped them into his cup. When his mixture was complete, he put the cup on the small fire.

He sat there on his haunches, watching and feeding the fire under his cup. Now and then, he looked up at me and smiled what seemed to be a knowing smile. Saltzman yelled for me to come up from the stream's bank to the cook's basha to eat. The inside doctor stayed at the water's edge watching his fire and the mixture in the tin cup.

The guides cut up the python into small squares and cooked them in a small wok. It was pure white meat with a delicious flavor. We pulled out the ivory chopsticks we had become adept with because we frequently put them to good use. They were farewell gifts from Ko Shin when we left the Third Regiment Headquarters. Everyone dipped into the pot together, and along with a small amount of rice, we had an incredible meal. We appreciated a tasty meal at this point in our travels through the wildest jungle in the world. Since we were running low on rice, this snake meat was also a significant addition to our food supply.

After I finished eating, I walked back down to check on the inside doctor who was still sitting by the stream, watching his fire. I looked down into the tin cup, and the contents were boiling away and looked like a thick liquid purple brew, now down to less than half a cupful.

In a few minutes, the inside doctor stood up and motioned for me to follow him. He walked up the embankment toward our basha. I motioned for Saltzman to come along with us. When we got to our basha, Duffy laid there still passed out, sound asleep. The inside doctor motioned for Saltzman and me to prop Duffy up. Then the doctor reached over, opened Duff's mouth, and poured the semi-hot purple potion down his throat. He motioned for us to lay him down again. We tied him back down with rattan, and the inside doctor bowed to us and walked away.

Saltz and I laid down, and with the first good full meal in days in our stomachs, we went to sleep.

The next morning, just after dawn, Saltz and I woke up, and Saltz said, "Let's get some breakfast."

Hearing that, Duffy tried to get up but found himself still tied to his bamboo bed.

I said, "How do you feel, Duff?"

Duffy responded, "I'm hungry."

Saltz and I untied him and helped him walk down to the guides' basha, where he ate hot rice and leftover python. After Duff finished breakfast, the head guide brought him the green bottle, and he drank a giant slug of quinine water. It stayed down, thank God.

That afternoon, Saltzman and I helped Duff walk around. Duffy needed to regain some strength in his legs before proceeding on our journey. We continued giving Duffy more quinine water throughout the rest of that day, and he kept it down. We knew when we gave him enough because when he drank the right amount of quinine water, his ears started ringing. In broken English and some sign language, the head guide informed us the inside doctor would return in the morning. So for the rest of the night, we got some rest.

The following morning, the inside doctor appeared out of the jungle and presented Duffy with a small paper bag filled with black-eyed peas. The doctor made it very clear that the peas were for Duffy and only Duffy. Then he told our head guide to prepare us to carry on with our expedition the next day after Duffy rested for one more day and night.

The inside doctor did not say goodbye. He turned and walked off into the jungle. As he faded into the wilderness, we thanked him for his willingness to help Duffy who desperately needed his help. This would not be the last miracle cure we would witness during our stay in Malaya.

CHAPTER 11

The Sixth Regiment

After another day's rest, on June 1st, we awoke at dawn and started again on our journey to the Sixth Regiment Headquarters to find J. Jack Bussy. We kept the pace slow for a while because of Duffy. It was apparent that the inside doctor's python potion did the trick because Duffy regained his strength and was back to his old regular rate of speed. To keep the fever from coming back, Saltz and I now and then gave him a slug of quinine water.

At 5:00 that afternoon, we stopped when we came to a small Sakai village on a riverbank. Again, the Sakai somehow knew we were coming. They were just as friendly as all the others. The elder Sakai of the tribe greeted us and presented us with a goat, which seemed to be the custom. A young woman with a big smile came running up and gave us each a pineapple, which also seemed to be the custom. They offered us one of their Sakai houses built well above the ground on top of a tree trunk like the dwellings Saltzman and I were familiar with from living with the Sakai months before.

Like the other Sakai, these Sakai here had never seen an American or a white person because they had never been out of their jungle habitat. Many of the Sakai followed us up the rattan ladder into our hut to get a better look at us. Our tree house filled to the danger point with all our Sakai friends visiting and watching our every move.

Later, the head guide came to tell me we were leaving in the morning and would go farther upriver to another Sakai village. I asked him to talk to the head of this tribe to see if they could find us some larger sampans for the next section of the trip. I wanted bigger sampans so everybody, including me with my long legs, could fit into them. He said he would try.

That night the Sakai killed, cleaned, cooked, and served us our gifted goat for dinner, which also seemed to be the custom. After dinner, we ate pineapple for dessert. We then went to bed for a good night's sleep in our tree house.

In the morning, a Sakai family with five children, boys and girls ages 5 to 15 all dressed in their typical loincloth attire, arrived to bring us food and watch us do whatever we were doing. For breakfast, they served us rice, two cooked chickens, and several kinds of peanuts. We enjoyed this hot, nourishing breakfast surrounded by an enthusiastic Sakai family. The Sakai here were just as fascinated with us as the others had been. We were as big a novelty to them as they were to us.

Like the other Sakai tribes, the Sakai children under five or six wore no clothes, and the adults wore almost nothing. Even children ages 8 to 14 wore only G-strings, and everybody, young and old, smoked handmade cigarettes.

In this village, besides their tree-trunk huts, there were also some additional 50-foot-long dwellings built on stilts. They appeared to be more like community buildings because they housed several families. One Sakai family we visited in one of the community houses owned two pets—a young owl and a black monkey—and both pets lived in the house.

We stayed with this tribe one night. The next morning, we walked down to the bank of the shallow river. Our two Chinese guides, the three of us, and several Sakai hopped into two large sampans the Sakai found for us. With the help of the Sakai, we made a lot of progress that day. They paddled us many miles north up the river, weaving through thick grasses and reeds most of the way. We arrived at another Sakai village that evening. As usual, all the Sakai in the tribe came down to the river to greet us. It was apparent they knew we were coming because they met us at the riverbank with loads of papaya, pineapples, and sugarcane. The Headman presented us with a goat just like the other tribes had done before, but this Headman added a big basketful of rice to go along with the goat.

It was late, so for dinner that night, we just ate various fruits and went to sleep on the bamboo floor of one of the Sakai houses built on top of a tree trunk.

The next morning, we woke up to watch two Sakai women pounding the rice the Headman gave us when we arrived. They used long poles to beat the rice and loosen the hulls. Then they poured the rice onto large, round, bamboo woven flats and threw it up in the air. The loose husks drifted away in the breeze, while the clean rice came back down on the bamboo flats. After the women finished cleaning the rice, they cooked it over a fire in front of our tree house. For breakfast, the two Sakai women served us our gifted goat they prepared earlier that morning along with the hot cooked rice, and we ate another excellent Sakai meal.

Later that day, the Chinese head guide told us we would have to move to a nearby farm to hide because an unusual number of Japanese soldiers had moved into the area looking for us. He also let us know we had left the jurisdiction area of Woo Ko Chung and Ah Sing of the Third Regiment and were now under the jurisdiction of the Sixth

Regiment. He said he already went ahead to the Sixth Regiment post number 162 to let them know we were here. Even after showing them the letters of protection from Woo Ko Chung, they still refused our admittance into the camp. He said he just received a new message from the commanding officer at post number 162 saying we were to remain here at the farmhouse until further notice. He said to rest a few days, and when things calmed down with the Japs, he would provide an Anti-Jap Army guerrilla guide and some guerrilla guards to escort us farther north to the Sixth Regiment Headquarters.

One day later, because of so many Japs in the area and our letters of protection from Woo Ko Chung, an English-speaking Chinese and a rifle-bearing guerrilla from the Sixth Regiment post number 162 joined us. We all settled in at the farmhouse, and our farmer host cooked us an excellent Chinese dinner of venison, eggs, rice, and turnips. After another delicious Chinese meal, we hit the sack for some much-needed sleep.

The Japs knew about this farm because they often came there and demanded free rice from our Chinese farmer host when they were in the area. The farmers, who were all Chinese, stored most of their rice where the Japanese could not see it. With the rice hidden, they would only have to give the Jap soldiers the small amount required to keep them appeased. They would sneak almost all the rest of their unknown rice to the Communist Anti-Jap Army.

The next day we moved to another nearby farmhouse because the young Chinese man who owned the house where we were staying had planned a wedding, and they were going to have a marriage feast the next day. It would have been too dangerous for us to attend the wedding party, so we had to move.

The next day we rested all day in our new Chinese farmhouse. That evening, our Chinese guide came to tell us the Anti-Jap Army commander at post number 162 had sent a new message saying we needed to remain at the farm for another day. Japanese soldiers were still moving into the area, and we could not leave. We could not have gone anyway because Duffy's fever was back. He had severe chills, and his chronic stomach pain caused by an unknown origin was worse than ever. I was in terrible shape myself. My never-ending GI trots returned several days before, and I also had a high fever. So Duffy and I took turns taking gulps of quinine water, trying to kill the malaria fever. We both felt awful.

That evening we got a new interpreter to replace the one who had just arrived. Kong, our new interpreter, was a one-lunged, chubby, round-faced young Chinese man with an amiable personality, and he spoke perfect English. Just as we got some useful information, the Chinese made another change and called Kong back to the guerrilla camp.

The commander replaced him with three Chinese Anti-Jap Army soldiers armed with Tommy Guns. One of them, who we soon named Fritz, spoke some English. The next morning, we received a message from the Commanding Officer at post number 162 saying the Japs had left the area. After another day's rest, Duffy and I felt well enough to travel.

We left the next morning. Fritz, the Chinese we just met who spoke some English, was now our new head guide. We headed out with Fritz, our two original guerrilla guides, and three extra armed soldiers provided to us by the Commander of post number 162.

We walked for four long hard hours in the rain and then stopped at a plantation worker's hut at the edge of a rubber estate. The farmer who lived there offered us some fresh coffee. He spoke only a little English, but he burst out with "English no good!" I guess he wanted us to know right away what his feelings were concerning the British and where he stood on that issue. After serving us a cup of coffee, he went over to the wall of his jungle cabin, took a shotgun down from its bamboo rack, walked out the door, and disappeared into the edge of the jungle. In a few minutes, the gun went off twice, and the farmer returned to the cabin with two black pheasants in hand. Smiling and a proud look on his face, he cleaned his birds. He skinned them first, and while we watched, he deboned them, keeping the birds in one piece, including the head. Our host cooked us a special meal of pheasant, rice, and hot Chinese tea after chopping them into chopstick-sized eating portions. He invited us to sleep there that evening, so we did.

We left the next morning and made some excellent progress for the next several days. It was now more comfortable walking through this area with plantations and animal trails, but we always had to deal with the leeches and mosquitoes. It was a never-ending battle with these parasites day in and day out. They were everywhere as we made our way through the Malayan rainforest.

We then received some information from a Chinese runner that slowed us down. The Japs heard we were in the area, and they were close by looking for us. If the Chinese Communists spotted any Japanese in our vicinity or received any information through their grapevine, the Chinese runners would bring us the information. Sometimes we would melt into the thick jungle to hide out until they told us it was clear to continue. Stopping and waiting several times a day became the routine, but we kept moving north. Zigzagging back and forth on our path and changing our course many times helped us avoid the Japs.

On June 20th, right at nightfall, Fritz led us out of the jungle into a small clearing where a large group of around 25 soldiers came at us from the other side. Fritz and the other guerrillas raised their Tommy Guns, ready to fire. Fritz shouted, "Guns down! It's a detachment of the Sixth Regiment!" And everybody lowered their arms.

Duffy said, "I thought it was all over for us."

"It would have been all over if those were Japs!" I replied. "Looks like we made it to the Sixth Regiment!"

Fritz introduced us to the Sixth Regiment Detachment Officers. First was a greasy looking Chinese named Ma-Ten who was Number One Captain of this Sixth Regiment Detachment. Next was Cheng Ping, a bucktoothed man with wire-rimmed glasses who turned out to be the Sixth Regiment's Propaganda Chief. Like many other young Chinese, both men were in their mid-20s, brainwashed by the Communist Party, and now young Communist leaders.

By the dim light of their oil lamp with Fritz as our interpreter, we sat in the clearing and spoke with the two Chinese officers. They wanted to know about our experiences in the jungle and asked some questions about America.

After answering their questions, my first question to them was, "Ma-Ten, do you have a radio?"

Ma-Ten answered, "No radio."

"Do you know where we can locate a radio transmitter?" I asked.

He answered, "No radio here. Only at Supreme Headquarters."

Then I asked about Bussy. I told Ma-Ten we had received a letter from Commander J. Jack Bussy. Woo Ko Chung, Number One Captain of the Third Regiment, gave us the letter, and we were on our way to find him. We discovered Bussy was very much out of favor with Ma-Ten and the Communist guerrillas of the Sixth Regiment Anti-Jap Army.

Ma-Ten told us that Bussy was an American Army Lieutenant who parachuted into Malaya with three Chinese assistants in December 1944 to gather information for the Allies about the Communist guerrilla movement. Then, with anger in his voice, he said the Anti-Jap Communist guerrillas asked Bussy many times to live at the Sixth Regiment Headquarters, but each time he refused. He told us Bussy lived on a plantation about 100 miles to the northeast owned by a very wealthy Chinese. He added that there was also a British Intelligence Detachment to the north with several officers and a few men who had parachuted into the bush a few weeks ago on a similar mission. Ma-Ten looked at me and declared that we should go north to the British Detachment instead of to Bussy.

When this discourse was over, the three of us looked at each other, and it was easy to see we were all thinking the same thing. We knew now that Bussy was not a Jap agent out to trap us as we had feared. Not liking the Communists was also in his favor because we also disliked the Communists. We told Ma-Ten we wanted to go where we could meet Commander J. Jack Bussy. He argued for half an hour, but he agreed to help us.

We left the next day to head north. With the help of Ma-Ten and 50 Sixth Regiment men, we made decent daily progress. But it was going to take three weeks of walking every day from dawn to dusk, only stopping in short-term jungle camps to hide from the Japs, to arrive at the plantation and J. Jack Bussy.

Ma-Ten said he heard through the grapevine that the Japanese were torturing farmers in the area and burning their houses to get information about the Sixth Regiment's location and the American Airmen who crashed in the jungle.

The Chinese Anti-Jap Army soldiers in the camps where we had stayed told us many horror stories about Japanese brutality. They would raid villages, burn down the houses, and rape all the women and children. The Japanese enjoyed torturing people for information, and after torturing them, they would chop off their heads in front of their families. These atrocities and other inhuman activities are why the Chinese and Malay natives grew to despise the Japanese.

The Japanese wanted to wipe out the Sixth Regiment Anti-Jap Army, and they were still looking for us, the American B-29 Airmen who bombed their homeland island. The Japs were all around us now. Although we encountered no shooting trouble with them, they kept us and the Sixth Regiment bouncing from one part of the jungle to another. Somehow, we were always where they were not.

Cheng Ping, the Propaganda Chief we came to call Ten Pin, was another Communist hypocrite. He was the former President of the National Youth Organisation of Malaya, and his father was a wealthy man. Ten Pin spent all his time writing Communist propaganda for the proletariat, but he never practiced what he preached. The bucktoothed Chinese always had two personal servants accompanying him, and they prepared his food, bathed him, and carried his luggage when he was on the trail. They even lugged his weapons for him.

A few days later while we were delayed in an extended campsite hiding from the Japs, several officers honored us. One of the Sixth Regiment's high-ranking officers named Lao Woo joined us after a long trek from the North. He brought a Chinese who looked and dressed like all the other Communist guerrillas, but he was a reporter from the Clandestine Communist Organization paper of Northern Malaya. He walked over, and while bowing to us, he said he wanted to interview us about our experiences in the jungle. But in the next hour, he did anything but that.

Saltzman, Duffy, and I sat down with the Chinese Communist reporter, along with Fritz, Ma-Ten, Ten Pin, Lao Woo, and one of his English-speaking officers named Wee Ming. The reporter's first question was this: "Why are there so many labor strikes in America?" That question and other following questions showed he was fishing for something to show that Communism was on the upsurge in the United States and would soon take over the country. He wanted to know why Americans discriminated against the Communists. I told him the only ones ever prosecuted were those convicted of subversive activity. Then he asked, "Why, if you don't persecute the Communists, hadn't we ever allowed any Communists to run for president?"

I explained that Earl Browder, a Communist candidate, ran for office every four years, but the people did not want him and never voted for him. I think this information surprised him.

The reporter dropped any pretense of interviewing us and began a long drawn out lecture on Communism. He declared that the Communist guerrilla movement would make sure Malaya became free from all outside influences after the war. We asked him if the Communists intended to achieve this freedom by force of arms because after the war, the American people would be tired of fighting. They would look with disfavor on any future Communist state set up on the theory that "might makes right."

The reporter declared, "The Communists do not intend to fight the British."

Ten Pin interrupted him and stated, "The guerrillas in the end will fight if necessary."

That ended the conversation with the reporter.

We learned who our new guide was for the next leg of our trip as we headed farther north from the Sixth Regiment Headquarters to the plantation and J. Jack Bussy. He was Lao Woo, the passionate Chinese Communist officer who just arrived in camp from the North. He was one of the highest-ranking officers of the Sixth Regiment and later became its Commander. After spending some time with Lao Woo, we also realized he hated white men because of the British.

With Lao Woo, our new fanatical Anti-Jap Army officer guide, along with an English-speaking guerrilla officer named Wee Ming and 15 armed guerrillas from Ma-Ten's Sixth Regiment, we headed north. This three-week journey was like every other trip we made during our months in the jungle. Leeches sucked our blood, and we went hungry. We were soaking wet from the almost constant rain, and the mosquitoes never stopped biting. Saltzman stubbed both his big toes so hard that the nails fell off just days later. Duffy still suffered from his fever and stomach pains. And I was still weak because of my bout with the GI trots and an occasional fever. But we pushed forward, closer and closer to Bussy and a radio. A significant difference now was that the Japs were always close by wherever we walked or camped. Even though it seemed as if the Japanese had information about our whereabouts, they could never pinpoint our exact location and capture us.

After two weeks of guiding us north through the Malayan jungle terrain and helping us dodge the Japs, Lao Woo announced he would head northeast to join the Second Detachment. He left us with Wee Ming as our guide and five armed guerrillas. We thanked Lao Woo for his help and bid him farewell. Wee Ming, who spoke fluent English, would guide us the rest of the way to the plantation to find J. Jack Bussy.

A few days later, as we moved ahead, we ran into trouble when we needed to cross the Pahang River near the Negeri Sembilan-Pahang border. The Japs were everywhere. The guerrillas did not know why so many Japanese were patrolling the Pahang River unless they were searching for us. We laid in the brush, hiding on the banks of the river all day. When night came, we slipped away in some pre-hidden dugout canoes and headed upriver. As we floated up the river, we were sometimes so close to the Japs we could hear their motor launch boats passing close by. We escaped with no detection or gunfire.

Dawn found us on the other side of the Pahang River, and Wee Ming guided us deep into the jungle, away from the Japs. We plodded ahead through the wet maze of green brush for two more days in the pouring rain. The leeches were everywhere. While walking in the pouring rain, I recalled what one guerrilla once said about the Malayan rain. "There are two seasons in Malaya. Rain and more rain. Winter monsoons from the north and summer monsoons from the south."

CHAPTER 12

Wong Cheong Yiat

Late in the afternoon on July 2nd, we broke out of the tangled dense jungle onto the edges of a large tapioca plantation. Our guerrilla guards were nervous because they said the tapioca fields were too open for safety. Wee Ming said the Japanese often traveled these plantation roads, and we needed to stay alert. He said the major highway between Kuala Lipis and Kuantan ran along the plantation's eastern edge. Many smaller roadways interlaced throughout the tapioca plantation where workers and sometimes Japanese soldiers traveled. Wee Ming and other Anti-Jap Communist officers were familiar with this plantation because they came here to get money and other supplies from the millionaire owner. We later learned that this vast tapioca estate spanned 4,000 acres.

Wee Ming said our destination was a plantation house about a mile away. He sent scouts ahead to check the area for Japanese soldiers. They came back in about an hour with an all-clear report. We waited another 30 minutes until dusk. Then Wee Ming guided us down a plantation roadway until it surprised us to see a very well-constructed frame house that looked similar to a barn because of its American barn-like architecture.

It was getting dark, so we crept up to the house. There was not a sign of life anywhere. Our guards slipped up the steps and rushed commando fashion straight through the front door with us following right behind them. Then there was silence, and we found ourselves in a dark, empty room. In the blackness, a match flared. We all jerked around in the direction of the flame with weapons ready. We couldn't see much, but it looked like a pair of hands attached to a small, slender body, holding up a Chinese oil lamp and lighting it with the match. With the dim glow from the flame in the lamp, we could make out the crouching figure of an ancient Chinese with a grin on his face. The old Chinese told Wee Ming we needed to be quiet until it was dark outside. We would be clear to go then because all the Japanese soldiers would leave the plantation at nightfall to return to their Army camp.

Wee Ming motioned to us to sit down and be quiet and wait for the Japs to leave for the night. We sat down on the dirt floor in the now pitch-black plantation house and dozed off while the guerrillas guarded the house outside. After a while, Wee Ming came in to tell us to come out. He pointed down a long path to a procession of torches winding its way up the hill. In the distance, coming toward us, we saw 10 or 12 rubber latex torches flaring in the night.

As they came closer, we could see they were Chinese. At the head of the column was a short, skinny, older Chinese man. He was wearing a white dress shirt, dark trousers, and a formal black jacket. When he walked closer, I could see his face. He appeared to be in his 50s, but it was difficult to tell the age of an older Chinese.

He walked up to me, bowed, and said, "Good evening. My name

164

is Wong Cheong Yiat. My brother and I own this plantation."

He spoke excellent English. He turned to a tall, very tough looking Chinese standing next to him and said, "I want to introduce you to Wong Soo."

Behind him were several Chinese bearers. Some had poles over their shoulders burdened with a large basket on each end, and others carried boxes and crates. Wong Cheong Yiat motioned for one of the taller Chinese to come forward and place a sizable old-fashioned looking trunk on the ground in front of us.

Wong Cheong Yiat made a ceremony of opening the trunk when he presented it to me. Because it was dark, I had to lean over to see what was in the chest, and it surprised me to find it was full of paper money. As I thanked him, he held up his hand and said, "This is a small token. There is a houseful of money if you need it."

I looked at him and smiled. My smile was saying thank you, and he understood. He took a small leather pouch from his pocket and poured 20 or more British gold sovereigns into my hand. "Wherever you go on the plantation here, do not let any Chinese see you. If someone does see you, they will recognize you because you are so tall. You must give him a gold coin and tell him, 'Be quiet.'" I did not know the value of a British gold sovereign, but in Japanese occupied Malaya, each one must have been worth a fortune.

He motioned another bearer forward who set two large baskets on the ground in front of us. One contained several pairs of new shoes of all different sizes, none large enough for me, however.

He said, "Do not worry if you cannot find shoes your size. I own a shoe factory, and I will get you a pair of shoes large enough to fit you."

The other basket contained clothes—fresh shirts, shorts, undershirts, trousers, and new socks. Since our clothes were rotting away, it was a welcome sight.

Next came a large crate filled with brandy bottles. He said they came from his brandy factory. And then there was another basket filled with dozens of packages of cigarettes.

Wong Cheong Yiat motioned for the other Chinese bearers to take their baskets into the house. He introduced us to his private cook and said he would prepare an enormous meal for us. While the cook went to work building a cooking fire, our gracious host motioned for us to go into the house with Wong Soo. We all sat on the dirt floor while Wee Ming stayed outside with the other guerrillas to stand guard.

A bearer brought us all a cup of brandy, and Wong Cheong Yiat brought out a new gold Swiss watch for each of us. He said, "I know America is going to win the war, and you can have anything you want. Everybody knows my brother Wong Cheong Kiat and me as the chicle kings of the world. We have exclusive rights from the Sultan of Pahang to tap the chicle trees in the entire state of Pahang, and we sell all our chicle to P. K. Wrigley in Chicago. The trees grow wild in the jungle, and we tap them like a rubber tree. Each tree must be close to 200 years old before it is large enough to tap. With the chicle, we make chewing gum."

He explained that no local Malay natives would go deep into the Malayan rainforest to tap the trees because the jungle was full of dangerous wild animals. They needed to import Chinese men from a specific province in China to come to Malaya to tap the trees. This need for Chinese men from China was one reason there were so many Chinese in Malaya. Many Chinese also came to Malaya in the mid-1800s to work in the tin mines, and more came later in the early 1900s to work on the British rubber plantations.

He said if you look into the jungle streams, you might see some white blocks two-feet square and six inches thick tied down with stakes under the water surface. He explained that these were blocks of raw rubber stored underwater. They could not ship the rubber out because of the Allied blockade that shut off all Malaya shipping. So they kept the rubber underwater to keep it preserved until it could be shipped.

Wong Soo was cold toward us. He sat stone-faced, watching from the corner of the room, and said nothing. His demeanor showed us he had doubts about us, or perhaps he disliked us. He was challenging to read. He was very tall for a Chinese, and we later learned he was from

Taiwan, which the Japanese considered their territory.

Wong Soo remained silent, but Wong Cheong Yiat opened more conversation by saying, "Tell me about the war. How is it going, and when will the Japanese be out of Malaya?" He said their current knowledge of the war was minimal outside of their territory. But what information they received came from the Japanese because Wong Soo was Japan's chief spy for the state of Pahang. The Japanese chose Wong Soo because he was Chinese from Taiwan, so they trusted him. Wong Soo was Wong Cheong Yiat's right-hand man, and he also controlled all the opium traffic in the state of Pahang.

As Saltzman, Duffy, and I sat there on the dirt floor sipping brandy with a Chinese millionaire and a Taiwanese who was a chief Japanese spy, I asked myself, "Had we walked all these miles to find this strange world?" At that moment, it all seemed bizarre.

Wong Cheong Yiat said because the Japanese soldiers left every evening after he fed them coffee and cakes, we could walk around the plantation without fear of the Japs. And besides that, Wong Soo would make sure of it. Wong Soo said nothing.

After an hour of brandy and talking about the war, we heard the head cook announce that dinner was ready. It was a 10-course meal with several prepared dishes, some with curry, some with peanuts, and all beautiful after months of jungle fare.

The dinner lasted more than two hours while we talked about the war and America. During the last brandy, Wong Cheong Yiat invited the three of us to his home on the plantation for dinner the following evening. He said we could not come until after dark because his house was close to Kuantan Road. We also needed to be sure all the Jap soldiers had gone for the night from the plantation.

When they left, we laid down on the dirt floor and slept with the satisfaction that we had found some good friends.

The next day we stayed inside, out of sight of the tapioca plantation workers, and rested. My diarrhea was awful and getting worse. The food was coming out as raw as it went in, and I lost weight each day. By this time, we all weighed less than 100 pounds and had become malnourished.

Wee Ming came over to us and said that later that evening, after dark, he would lead us with armed men down to Wong Cheong Yiat's main plantation house. As it became dark, we started down a narrow path alongside a plantation road between tall tapioca plants on the right and the main Kuantan Road on the left. On the way, we passed the Plantation Office Building on the left, which looked like an American roadside motel with a U-shaped driveway in front. It was large enough for four or five good-sized rooms. We also passed several small worker-huts along the way, but we did not see any of the workers or occupants.

Wee Ming led us up to the front of a small farmhouse, Wong Cheong Yiat's main house, and then waited for us outside with the other guerrillas to guard the house. Wong Cheong Yiat came to the door to greet us. Wong Soo stood in the background, scowling at us with his severe features. Wong Cheong Yiat said he wanted us to meet his wife and their young son. He took us back to a small bedroom where he introduced us to a pretty, young Chinese girl in her 20s. She could not speak English. As was the custom, she would not sit with us at the dinner table. Wong Cheong Yiat later told us she was one of his three wives and that Chinese men could have as many wives as they wished if they could afford them.

We moved back to the dining room, maybe 20 feet by 30 feet in size, at the front part of the small five-room farmhouse. Wong Cheong Yiat invited us to sit at a round table in the center of the room. Duffy, Saltzman, and I sat down, and then Wong Soo and Wong Cheong Yiat joined us at the table. There was not much furniture in the house. Everything felt and looked almost like a typical small farmhouse in the United States.

As soon as we sat down, Wong Cheong Yiat said, "Now tell us about the progress of the war."

Without notice, five young Chinese boys, about 12 to 14 years old, trotted in a single file out of one of the side rooms and set a glass of white wine down in front of each of us.

Wong Cheong Yiat picked up his glass and proposed a toast. "America soon wins the war!"

As soon as the empty glasses hit the table, the five young Chinese boys came running out. Each one picked up an empty glass and ran back to the other room.

Then Saltzman said, "We have been in the jungle, running and hiding from the Japanese, since January 11th, and we have no more current information than what we received through the grapevine, and that is not much information at all."

Saltzman started to tell them about the B-29 bombing raids we made on the Japanese Islands when, with no apparent signal, the five young boys came running back in, each with another glass of white wine. They set a wine glass in front of us and ran back out of the room in a single file. No one made a move, and Wong Cheong Yiat continued talking about the war. So I raised my glass in a toast to Wong Cheong Yiat and Wong Soo. I said, "Since the closest help from any Allied troops is more than 2,000 miles away, we very much need your help. Thank you for helping us evade the Japanese Army."

We all downed the wine, and when the glasses hit the table, the five young boys ran into the room, picked up the glasses, and trotted out in their usual single file.

Wong Soo continued to say nothing, but Wong Cheong Yiat kept up with question after question about the B-29s and the war. The five young boys came trotting back into the room and set a cup in front of each of us. I looked down at my cup, and there was a raw egg floating on top of boiling coffee. Duff and Saltz looked down at the eggs cooking in their cups, and then we all three looked up at each other and smiled. Meanwhile, Wong Cheong Yiat kept talking about the war and how he was sure America would win the war, and he reassured us he would give us anything we wanted. He wanted us to tell him more about the war and America, so our inquiring host continued to talk and ask questions while our eggs continued to cook in our cups.

Without a visible signal of any kind, the five boys trotted back in, picked up the coffee cups no one had touched, and took them out.

Wong Cheong Yiat said two things helped him keep a good relationship with the Japanese. First, he gave the Japanese hot coffee and cakes every day. Second, his right-hand man, Wong Soo, reported all the area's activity to the Japanese Commander. Wong Cheong Yiat also said Wong Soo had a close relationship with the Japanese Commander. There was even one incidence when they went together to have their syphilis treated.

The five young boys trotted back into the room again with five fresh cups of coffee with new raw eggs floating in them. Saltzman and Duffy looked at the cups, and Wong Cheong Yiat kept right on talking.

Duff said, "I don't know what you are going to do, but I'm going to drink mine."

When he picked up his cup, the two Chinese picked up their cups, and we all downed the coffee and the poached egg. Our two Chinese hosts did not think we liked it, and they would not drink unless we did.

Wong Cheong Yiat was an unforgettable character. He was a short, slight, Caspar Milquetoast type looking man with eyes that always blinked. By habit, Wong Cheong Yiat pulled his lips with his long, slender hands that showed he had been working with his mind and not his hands over his past 50-plus years. He was the Head Man at this estate, and with his brother the head man of everything in the state of Pahang, he had taken a chance on Jack Bussy. They supported Bussy because he was an American and not a German or a Jap. He also had to keep the Japanese and the Communist guerillas happy.

Wong Cheong Yiat's estate ownership forced him to help the Japanese because he wanted to keep his business operating, which made him appease their every desire. Anything they wanted, they could have. The Japs took almost his entire fleet of trucks except one he used at his sawmill to move lumber to make boats. And he kept a few at the plantation. He sold his tapioca to the Japanese for $42.40 per unit, and they resold it in town for $550 or more per unit. Slight profit!

When the Communist Anti-Jap Army came to him demanding another $10,000 payment, he gave it to them, even though he had already contributed more than $1 million to the Central Military

Committee over the last year.

This terrified Chinese millionaire thought if he did not give the Japanese everything they wanted, they might confiscate all his property and take over his plantations. Or someday they might come unannounced to investigate the estate and capture Bussy.

It scared him to tell the Anti-Jap Communist Army they could not have this or that because he knew they knew he also helped the Japanese Army. The Communist guerrillas killed anyone who was a traitor to their Anti-Jap Communist Party. Wong Cheong Yiat knew they were letting him slide because he supported them.

Wong Cheong Yiat was also afraid not to help us because he feared the Allies would say he did not support the Americans. He thought if the Americans heard he had not supported us, it would hurt his sales in the United States after the war. Wong Cheong Yiat was in a continuous circle of appeasement, and he did it well.

Since Wong Cheong Yiat employed Wong Soo, a Japanese spy, he was privy to some information about the Japanese Army's movements in the area. He told us the Japs were evacuating the central part of Kuala Lumpur and did not have any tanks left there. The Japanese Army sent most of their tanks north to Siam and were now dispersing the few soldiers left in the area to camps all around Malaya. He also said, with disgust, that the 2,000 to 3,000 Japanese soldiers stationed in Kuantan were cutting down all the rubber trees near the town to use for firewood.

Wong Cheong Yiat ended the night by emphasizing his necessity to donate to the Communist Anti-Jap Army in order to survive. He also made it clear that he did not like them or what they stood for, and most of what he did was provide them with rice. He added that he hoped the Allies would soon rid Malaya of the Japanese.

The Chinese millionaire's hands were full taking care of J. Jack Bussy and company while appeasing the Japanese Army and the Communist Anti-Jap Army. And now we were here. He was busy with a lot of balls in the air, and he was always nervous.

CHAPTER 13

Bussy

On July 7th after a six-month jungle trek and five hours of brisk walking from the tapioca plantation, Saltzman, Duffy, and I, along with our Chinese Communist Anti-Jap Army guide Wee Ming and his men, arrived at Commander J. Jack Bussy's jungle camp.

Bussy came flying out of a small building with three young Chinese men running close behind him. He shouted, "Damn! Am I glad to see you! What the hell took you so long to get here? Don't you know I have been waiting since January? And I have not seen or spoken to an American since last December. Come on in here. I'll grab a bottle of brandy, and we'll celebrate."

I could see right away that Commander J. Jack Bussy was an interesting character. He was wearing an Australian hat and shirt, American Army pants, and American Army issued boots. The man looked like he had not bothered to shave for a week. In his right hand was a Thompson machine gun. He had a carbine strapped over his shoulder, a .45 caliber pistol holstered around his waist, and a machete and two hand grenades clipped to his belt. A cigarette hung from his lips. Bussy looked like he was always ready for trouble or perhaps ready to make trouble.

Bussy said, "Sit down, and I'll pour us all a brandy."

As he was pouring, I asked, "Who are the boys here with you?"

He answered, "This big boy is Yapper. Here we have Khaki, and over here we have Angry. These three fine Chinese boys parachuted in with me."

"Nice to meet you, boys," I said, greeting all of them.

Then, looking at Bussy, I said, "Commander Bussy, this is Wee Ming, our guide from the Sixth Regiment. Wee Ming would like to take care of some business so he can be on his way. Wee Ming tells us you agreed with the Sixth Regiment to pay them with guns and money for delivering us to you."

Bussy walked over to shake Wee Ming's hand and said, "It's a pleasure to meet you, Wee Ming. I have your money right here."

Bussy pulled a big wad of bills out of his pocket and asked Khaki to bring him his leather bag. Bussy opened a small pouch from inside his leather bag, spilled 15 gold coins onto the table, and said, "Here are 30,000 Jap dollars, 3,000 Thai dollars, and 15 gold pieces. That should cover it."

"What about the guns?" Wee Ming asked.

"We are waiting for Allied Headquarters in Ceylon to make the parachute drop," Bussy answered. "You will receive the carbines I promised when we receive the carbines from Ceylon. You will have to wait, just like us."

"Seventy-five guns, 25 for each man. That was our deal. We will wait to hear from you," Wee Ming said with a look on his face that said, "I will be back with the Sixth Regiment if we don't hear from you soon."

Saltz, Duffy, and I then gave Wee Ming our pistols as we promised to do when we arrived at our destination.

Wee Ming said, "Major Humphrey, Lieutenant Duffy, Lieutenant Saltzman, thank you for keeping your word. I am grateful."

"Thank you for your help, Wee Ming. We wish you the best," I said. Wee Ming turned, gave us a wave goodbye, and left to go back to the Sixth Regiment.

After Wee Ming left, I asked Bussy, "Can you make good on your promise?"

Bussy answered with a smile, "You let me worry about that."

That answer worried me, but I let it go so we could move on to talking about our plans to meet a submarine for our escape from Malaya.

Bussy's camp was a first-rate jungle camp, as jungle camps go, with around 25 delightful Chinese lads living there who took good care of us. We could tell the boys liked their music because there was a phonograph that played Malay and Chinese music at full volume. It seemed out of place deep in the wildest jungle in the world and was also annoying. There was a 60-foot-long bamboo hut with a long continuous bed down one side. A few bamboo walls sectioned off several rooms, making one room for Bussy and one room for Khaki, Angry, and Yapper. There was a third room for some women who lived there to cook and wash clothes. Near the camp, there was a fresh flowing stream that was convenient for cleaning and cooking.

There was even some mysterious intrigue brewing in the camp among the Chinese because of a young Chinese man who just arrived from Kuala Lumpur. Bussy suspected he was a Japanese spy.

Duffy moaned and said, "Hey, Bussy, do you have anything here that might help these stomach pains? My stomach is killing me."

Duffy had been suffering from stomach pains almost every day since we bailed out of the *Postville Express*. He did not know if the problem came from the side injury he received when bailing out, his malaria, or what he feared most—his appendix. Duffy always feared the side pain was because of an injured appendix. If it ever burst in the middle of the jungle where there were few doctors, he knew it would be fatal. With his relentless stomach pains and the usual and sometimes severe malaria fever, Duffy was in terrible shape most of the time. I worried that if he were not under the care of a doctor soon, he would die in this jungle as Hansman did.

Bussy gave him a stiff dose of sulfathiazole, and he also switched him to Atabrine instead of quinine water for malaria. Because of Wong Cheong Yiat and his brother, Bussy could keep his camp well stocked with medical supplies.

We talked for a while about the camp and a little about our experiences in the jungle. As Commander Bussy poured us another glass of brandy, I asked, "Are you in the Army, Bussy?"

He said, "Yes, assigned to the OSS, the Office of Strategic Services, Intelligence."

Bussy told us he parachuted in with the three Chinese boys on December 7th to contact a British officer named Pat Noone. When Singapore fell to the Japs, Noone was left behind and was now hiding in a Sakai village somewhere. Bussy hoped he could still find him living with one of the Sakai tribes, but he had not located him so far.

"When we came in," Bussy explained, "the damn British Liberator pilot dropped us 86 miles from our scheduled drop-off location, and only half our equipment landed with us. He dropped the other half, including a second radio, who knows where in the jungle. The good news is we touched down in the middle of a millionaire's plantation and a friendly millionaire to boot. So here we are."

I asked Bussy, "In your letter, you said you were operating under an alias, Commander J. Jack Bussy. What is your actual name?"

"Franklin Bithos," he said with a proud look on his face. "Born and raised in Marysville, Missouri."

"Bithos. What's a Bithos?" Saltz blurted out in a bit of a drunken slur.

"Here, let me pour you another brandy, Saltz. It's time to celebrate," Bussy shouted.

We all laughed and started to talk over our plan for a submarine to pick us up when Bussy said he had already thought out a plan for us.

We listened, and his idea sounded doable but dangerous. We also needed to contact the Allied Forces at Headquarters in Ceylon first.

"Bussy, where is your radio?" I asked.

"The radio is right over there in the shed, but it can't transmit, only receive."

I snapped back with, "How the hell were you planning on contacting a sub or HQ for our escape out of here?"

"Are any of you guys handy with a radio?" Bussy asked. "It comes and goes. Maybe we can get it working."

Saltzman answered, "Hump, I'll look at it."

"You a radioman?" Bussy asked.

"Flight engineer, but I looked over our radioman Mick's shoulder enough to know a bit about radios."

"Where's Mick?" Bussy asked.

"Missing!" Saltzman burst out.

"Sorry. How many in your crew are missing?" asked Bussy.

"I am still missing eight members of my crew." With some anger in my voice, I said, "Based on your letter to us saying there was a radio here in your camp, we came here instead of going north to the Second Detachment with Lao Woo. Have you ever transmitted with this radio?"

"Yes. I think we can get this thing going," Bussy responded. "But who is Lao Woo, and what and where is this Second Detachment?"

I explained to Bussy, "Lao Woo is a high-ranking Sixth Regiment officer who guided us halfway here and then went 100 miles farther north to his Second Regiment Detachment. A few weeks ago, some British officers with several men parachuted into the Chinese Communist Anti-Jap Army Second Detachment camp to organize the Anti-Jap Army for when the British returned."

"Wow! I didn't know that," Bussy responded.

Bussy told us the radio was not transmitting out, but we could receive some news at a frequency of 6210. He asked Angry to bring in the radio, and we dialed in the receiver to 6210, drank some more brandy, and listened. Borneo's war news that day sounded good for the Allies, and Borneo was only 375 miles from Malaya. At least we knew the Allies were winning and moving closer.

Some Chinese plantation coolies arrived with more than a dozen live chickens and several boxes filled with our gifts from Wong Cheong Yiat. We ate chicken for dinner, and the entire camp ate chicken with us. We also supplied everybody with cigarettes from the gift boxes we received from Wong Cheong Yiat. It appeared that everybody smoked in Malaya. With the delivery were also two large boxes of cigars. After dinner, Saltzman, Duffy, and I enjoyed some more of that beautiful tasting brandy and a superb cigar with our new friend Commander J. Jack Bussy. Duffy could not drink much brandy because of his stomach issues, but he sure enjoyed one of Wong Cheong Yiat's excellent cigars.

The next morning, I dipped my face in the refreshing stream to wake up after our night of celebration. Then I soaked my feet. They looked like they were trying to heal and get back to normal. The deep holes in the balls of my feet were now starting to fill back in. My big toe no longer had an infection, but I still did not have a big toenail. One of Saltzman's toes, now infected, was in awful shape. He joined me on the bank of the stream and soaked his feet, hoping to ease the pain.

Wong Cheong Yiat gave us at least six pairs of pre-war shoes, but none of them were big enough for me. He also sent us each a towel, several pairs of socks, new trousers, two shirts each, and more shoes. Duff and Saltz both found a nice pair of shoes, but I still wore Chinese handmade shoes. We needed the shirts and pants since ours were all rotted. My pants were too short, but they were new and clean, and it thrilled me to have them. Wong Cheong Yiat supplied us with all we needed, and money was available in any amount we needed. All we needed to do was ask.

Bussy's radio operated on batteries. There were two batteries in the camp, so they exchanged the two batteries. While one was charging, the other was in use, and the one full-time generator always needed to be in working condition to keep the batteries charged. Angry, Bussy's man trained to operate the radio, could never have it working on the specified dates and times pre-scheduled by Ceylon to transmit out. Ceylon expected to receive these messages from Bussy on these selected dates. Still, since the day he parachuted into the jungle last December, Bussy could make no scheduled contacts with Allied Headquarters in Ceylon.

A gasoline engine, parachuted in with Bussy and his three boys, powered the generator that charged the batteries. The plane dropped two gasoline generators, but only one survived. The generator engine ran but did not sound right to me. If we could repair the radio transmitter in time or at the right time for the scheduled outgoing message, we needed to ensure the generator engine worked to keep the batteries charged.

The next day was the scheduled date Ceylon would listen for Bussy's radio message. Since the radio never worked before on the scheduled dates and never made even one scheduled contact with Ceylon for the last 10 months, Bussy and Angry were not optimistic. But we continued to work on the radio and the generator and would try again tomorrow.

On July 8th, Saltz and I spent all morning trying to fix the generator motor. Saltz boasted it would be a simple undertaking since he was an aeronautical engineer, but I told him my Model T experience in high school was more helpful. He might take a 2,000-horsepower aircraft engine apart, but I would be better at taking a small gasoline engine like this apart.

There were a few wrenches and pliers fastened to the engine, and we went to work. We took the cylinder head off to find both the intake and exhaust ports closed. The exhaust port was 95 percent closed with carbon, so it was a miracle it ran at all. We cleaned it and checked the timing and magneto, and when we reassembled it, it ran like a top. I think we impressed the Chinese who were standing around watching us.

After we finished with the generator, Saltzman went to work on the radio. After a while, the radio transmitter was functioning, but only off and on—sometimes off and sometimes on.

The time came to make the scheduled radio contact with Ceylon. "How's it looking, Saltz?" I asked.

"Not good, Hump," Saltz said, looking down at the radio. "I think this transmitter has bit the dust. We can receive the news on the 6210 frequency, but that's it. No messages are going out with this baby."

"It doesn't look like we will plan the escape from Malaya with this radio," I remarked. "I think we will need to go to the Second Detachment. If the British officers are there, they will have a radio."

"I'll go," Bussy blurted out. "I need to contact South East Asia Command in Ceylon to give them coordinates and dates for some parachute drops. I also need to order a new radio and generator, some more supplies, and those 75 carbines to keep Wee Ming and the Sixth Regiment off my back."

"I'll go, too," I added. "I will contact the 20th Bomber Command and give them our names and serial numbers. And Duff, I will be sure they know we must get medical care for your stomach and chest injuries ASAP. During our absence, Duffy, you and Saltz will oversee the camp."

"We will need some Communist guerrillas to guide us there," Bussy added. "I will send Khaki and two boys to the Sixth Regiment camp about two hours south of here to see if they can find us two guides. I will have them meet us at the plantation house tomorrow. We can go ahead to the plantation to put some supplies together and wait for them there."

Bussy and I made plans to go to the tapioca plantation the next day to find the supplies we needed and wait for Khaki to bring us the guerrilla guides to take us to the Second Detachment.

In the morning, Bussy supplied us with .30 caliber carbines, and then Bussy, Yapper, and I left at about 11:00 to walk back to the plantation.

Hiking to the plantation house from Bussy's camp took around five hours. Bussy's route used animal trails, and the terrain was up and down hills all the way. When it rained, the path was muddy and slippery, but overall, it was not too bad of a trip.

We arrived at a farmhouse at the edge of the plantation in the late afternoon. We stayed there until later when we could cross the road in the dark and then walk on to the plantation house. It rained hard the entire way to the plantation.

On the shortcut route Bussy chose and just before reaching the road that would take us to the house, we needed to cross a ditch. It was around 50 feet deep and 40 feet across. Some fallen trees crisscrossed one another at all angles, creating a log bridge across the ravine. Yapper started running across the ditch, jumping from one tree trunk to another in his bare feet and reached the other side without falling.

I crossed deep ditches like this many times on our long walk through the jungle. We went across ravines a lot wider and deeper than this one, and the logs were always slippery from the endless rains. The trips across those logs high above the bottom of the canyons 150 feet below were frightening. We often sat down with one leg on each side, straddling a log, and scooted across on our rear ends while hanging on for dear life. The Chinese guerrillas would trot right by us at a rapid pace from log to log while laughing at us all the way. However, it was a serious matter for us because we knew if we fell and broke a leg or hurt ourselves, it was all over. We were deep in Japanese-occupied Malaya, and the only help we would ever receive from the Japs was a bullet in the head.

Once earlier on our jungle trek, we sat down to rest after crossing a log-covered ravine. Saltzman looked at me and said, "Hump, after all this experience, I am going to show off and make some big money when I go home. There is a wooden fence in my backyard, and if I make it back, I will take the garden hose and wet the fence down. I will invite everyone in the neighborhood over to make bets on whether I can run along the top of the wet wooden fence from one end to the other without slipping off."

Then Saltzman looked over at me and smiled like he was already counting all that money he was going to win.

Bussy, Yapper, and I crossed the ravine and walked a few miles up the road. We arrived at the plantation manager's home where there was a welcome cup of hot coffee waiting for us. Soaked head to toe, the coffee refreshed us.

From there, we took some latex rubber torches and walked another 30 minutes on a plantation road. This road went all the way around the rectangular-shaped, 4,000-acre plantation. There was a tapioca field on one side of the road, and on the other side was a thick wall of jungle and swamp. On down the road, we passed a building they called House #24, one of the worker bunkhouses, but we did not see any workers anywhere. We wondered why it was empty.

We arrived at the same barn-like house at the corner of the field where we met Wong Cheong Yiat and later would meet Khaki and our new Communist guides. The Chinese guards prepared chicken, eggs, and rice, and we sat down to an excellent Chinese meal. I was now enjoying food that was a welcome change from the diet we lived on for most of the last six months in the jungle.

We slept until 11:00 in the morning when Khaki arrived without guides but with a messenger from the Communist Anti-Jap Army. Khaki said the guerrillas would arrange for a guide and an armed escort to take us to the Second Detachment, but they wanted to meet with us first. We told the messenger we would like to meet and leave for the Second Detachment ASAP. He left with our message at 11:30.

The messenger came back around 6:00 p.m. and told us a Sixth Regiment commander said it would take several days to make our trip arrangements, and they would be back in touch with us. We then put some pressure on the messenger by telling him we needed to leave soon. He left with the message and returned two hours later. He said they held a meeting and decided it was impossible to let us go, but they would write their Number One Captain and ask him to come here to meet us.

We told him to go back and tell them we needed to see the Second Detachment British officers ASAP about some guns. We would also talk to them about sending some weapons for them while we were there. That impressed him because Bussy stood there dripping with pistols and hand grenades, and both of us had new American-made carbines strapped over our shoulders.

The messenger came back in a few hours and said that after another meeting, they decided we could leave the day after tomorrow. He said to walk to the camp house at the 74-mile post where we would meet the Number One Captain.

A few hours later, Wong Cheong Yiat arrived at the plantation house in his Austin convertible to see us. We told him where we were going and said we would leave Duffy and Saltzman in charge at Bussy's camp. He told us to be careful, and if we needed any money, he could give us plenty, as much as we wanted. Wong Cheong Yiat did not keep any records of what he gave Bussy or me. He was doing it for the Allies to help win the war, and he wanted to stay in good favor with the Americans.

Our millionaire friend stayed for a while to visit with us. He told us about the Japs coming to his plantation every evening for free coffee and cakes. He said they always left their guns in their trucks because he told them, "This is a very good, safe place." Then his eyelids fluttered, and he pulled his lips until they were almost bleeding. He laughed and took another drink of wine. Wong Cheong Yiat gained the trust of the Japanese with coffee and cakes, and he was proud of his brilliant arrangement.

Wong Cheong Yiat, with the satisfaction of a wealthy man, spoke of his many businesses. He started from the bottom and became successful. He was now a satisfied and wealthy man. His neat white shirts, Chinese trousers, and an expensive black coat, frayed around the lapels because of four years of Jap occupation, made him look like an entrepreneur of impeccable standing. He was a Milquetoast-type looking man, but he was far from being a shortsighted man. Wong Cheong Yiat was a creative, capable, intelligent, understanding, and impressive individual. He was also an intuitive man who had foreseen the effects of the Japanese occupation from the very beginning. He had already banked almost his entire wealth in New York City because of his foresight, and the rest was in gold buried on his plantation.

His brother, Wong Cheong Kiat, known as the Jelutong King of the World, owned a great deal of jelutong raw rubber that he stored underwater in the jungles of Malaya. The raw rubber was ready to be sold after the war. He also held an abundant supply of old rubber already prepared for shipment. The Sultan of Pahang gave his rubber factory a special permit to collect all the rubber in Pahang. There was much more rubber available to tap from the rubber trees than his factory could ever use.

With pride, Wong Cheong Yiat said he was extremely wealthy. Workers on his plantation received 10 times the pay of a Jap officer. He said he sold goods at the store on his estate at a loss because "people talk too much." He kept everybody loyal and quiet with money and rice.

When we finished our engaging and friendly conversation, Wong Cheong Yiat climbed back into his Austin convertible and went home.

On July 11th, I celebrated my sixth month in the jungle. We started with five of us and went down to three. I felt fortunate to be alive. So far, by the grace of God and with the help of Malay natives, Chinese Communist guerrillas, Sakai natives, and a Chinese millionaire named Wong Cheong Yiat, we—Saltzman, Duffy, and I—had survived in the Japanese-occupied Malayan rainforest for six months.

It would be two days before we left. So while we waited, Bussy and I went wild boar and elephant hunting. We started down the path toward our hunting grounds. When we stepped up on a log to survey the area, we saw a huge, proud-looking Bengal tiger in front of us about 10 feet away. He saw us and bounded into the tapioca and out of sight. We went over to look at his tracks. His paw prints were about five inches across.

As we moseyed down a path in the tapioca field, I was thinking everything over. After seeing Wong Cheong Yiat's Austin earlier, I asked Bussy, "Do you think our good millionaire friend would allow us to borrow his Austin to drive to our meeting at the 74-mile post?"

"I don't know. Let's ask him this evening," Bussy said with a smile.

Yapper said the elephants came out of the jungle every afternoon at a nearby location. We waited there in the tapioca for some time before we heard them trumpeting and crashing through the brush. Around 10 elephants broke out at the jungle's edge, but only one came close enough for any of us to take a shot. Yap shot at a huge one, but all it did was grunt and walk away. A .30 caliber carbine is not much of an elephant gun.

After our unsuccessful hunting trip, we waited until just after dark and then walked up to Wong Cheong Yiat's home on the east road a mile north of the plantation house where we were staying. With his plantation house on the main Kuantan-Kuala Lipis Road, we still needed to be alert for Japs who could come down the road even though it was after dark. We had grown accustomed to being mindful and on the lookout for the Japanese soldiers. I was at a point now where it almost became natural to be on alert for the Japs.

When we arrived, Wong Cheong Yiat invited us in and gave us each a glass of his excellent brandy. When we talked with him about driving his Austin up to the 74-mile post for our meeting, he became more nervous by the minute. While he thought it over, the worried Wong Cheong Yiat pulled more and more skin off his lips. After several more minutes of discussion, there were a few minutes of silence. Then he turned to Wong Soo and ordered him to put his Japanese issued license plates on the Austin. There was one red star on each of the two license plates. The Japanese gave Wong Soo these plates to use when he traveled on his Japanese spy business. They allowed Wong Soo to go anywhere, and they assured us that with these plates on the Austin, the Japanese would leave us alone.

That night we walked back to Bussy's camp to get some other supplies we wanted and talk about our plans. At dinner, Bussy said, "Duff, see that Chinese over there by the fire? I think he might be a spy for the Japs. Monitor him. Don't let him leave this camp."

They informed me weeks later that they found out for sure he was a Japanese spy. Saltzman was the one who would end up executing him with a shot in the chest.

The next day, we left Duffy and Saltzman in charge and took Khaki and Yapper back to the plantation house. We needed to prepare for our meeting with the Number One Captain at the 74-mile post.

Our transportation was a 1941 convertible Austin 8 Tourer that seated two in the front seats and two in the rear seat, so only four could go. Bussy and I jumped in the back, Khaki hopped in the passenger seat, and Yapper got behind the wheel. It was a 35-minute drive to the 74-mile post. We were almost there when a big black panther ran from the side of the road, jumped right over the front hood, and bounded into the jungle. That incredible leap gave me chills. The excitement never ends when you are in the Malayan rainforest.

When we reached the 74-mile post, we drove about 200 yards into the plantation where we found the house where we were to meet the Number One Captain. We looked around and knocked on the door, but no one was there—no contact man, no guide, and no Number One Captain. We thought they would come later, so we settled in and rested. When late evening came and still no one showed, we stayed there to sleep for the night in case they were running late.

In the morning, we went outside to have another quick look around, and we saw three British Mosquito Bombers fly over. They came from the east, which meant Borneo. After all these months of waiting and hoping for the end of the war, it was a very welcome sight.

Bussy sent Yapper out to buy some food. After Yapper left, some Malay workers came by the house. Khaki talked with them, and they said they worked for the government and were there to repair the telephone lines. Bussy and I hid behind the house while Khaki kept them distracted. They did not see us and soon left. A few hours later, a Chinese man came walking down the road. We watched him as he walked by. It seemed like he kept glancing in our direction. We sent Khaki out to talk to him, but the man disappeared into the jungle before Khaki could speak with him. We became suspicious and decided it was time to clear out. Nobody was showing up at this 74-mile post house, and there was a big reward for anyone who helped the Japanese capture us, so we could not take any chances.

We walked across the road into the jungle to wait for Yapper to return. As we waited, we thought about the mysterious man who walked by and the government telephone line workers. Were they notifying the Japs about our location? Were the Japanese troops in the area and on our trail? We did not know, but we always needed to be thinking of options and be on high alert in case they were. An hour later, Yapper came back with the car and told us the people in the village said they heard through the grapevine that a Japanese general had sent 5,000 Japanese soldiers on an expanded search with orders to find us and bring us in. The Japanese Army wanted to capture us, and they were not giving up.

We continued to wait for the Number One Captain a while longer. A runner came with instructions from the Number One Captain instructing us to go to the 79-mile post and remain there until our new guides arrived. We were unsure what to make of this unusual change in plans. We drove to the 79-mile post, parked the car behind a small building, and hid in the brush to wait.

At about noon, Wong Cheong Yiat pulled up to the 79-mile post in one of his other cars. He delivered a letter from Lao Woo, our old guide, who was now the Number One Captain at the Second Detachment Regiment. The letter said Lao Woo would send two guerrilla guides to the plantation to escort us to his Second Detachment Regiment. A British Major would wait for us there with a radio.

"Bussy, I think I found my radio."

"Yes," Bussy replied. "Now, all we have to do is get there."

CHAPTER 14

Trek to Second Detachment

We all drove back to the plantation house to wait. The two guides Lao Woo provided for us arrived at the plantation in the late afternoon, and we planned to leave that night.

After speaking with our guides, we planned to walk up to the 74-mile post that night and sleep there. Bussy and I would walk through the jungle for 10 hours the first day and eight hours the next day. We hoped to arrive at the Second Detachment camp sometime the second night.

Bussy and I made all the preparations for the trip that evening. Bussy said eggs were nutritious and easy to pack, so we bought around

50 eggs from the local farmers at $5.00 apiece. Wong Cheong Yiat's cook hard-boiled them for us to take on the trip.

Because Wong Cheong Yiat allowed us to use his car earlier, Bussy and I, after some discussion, went back to Yiat's house again. We asked if we could borrow a truck or a lorry from the plantation barn to use for part of the first night's journey up the road. At first, Wong Cheong Yiat objected, as usual, but he agreed and went away, pulling more skin from his lips.

The truck was going to save us a lot of time. If we took it to the 61-mile post, it would save us hours of walking in the jungle and hiding from the Japs we might encounter along the way. At about 2:00 in the morning, a plantation lorry showed up with the plantation manager in the passenger seat. The driver said he would first have to take a drive to check the road before we left.

When he returned an hour and a half later, the Chinese guerrillas loaded the truck with our supplies. Bussy and I, two armed guerrillas for extra protection, and our two new Chinese guerrilla guides with rifles climbed into the back of the truck. We told the driver we wanted to go to the 61-mile post. The driver said there was a kampong at the 61-mile post, and he would take us there.

We rode around 40 minutes up the road and then made an unscheduled stop at the 74-mile post to drop off the plantation manager. He wanted off because he thought there were too many Japanese in the area ahead to go farther.

We made it to the village at the 61-mile post, and the driver let us off with our supplies. The ride beat 16 or more hours of walking in the jungle dodging Japs. After our drop-off, we walked about an hour until, at dawn, we were back in the bush off the road and safer. We set up camp near the town of Jerantut. A Chinese man arrived from town to tend to the small jungle garden he owned nearby. We gave him $100, and the guides told him he could not leave until after we left the area. All he said was, "Okay."

We slept during the day, and early that night, we walked down to a Sakai camp where our Chinese guide introduced us to Pongulu, the

Chief of the Sakai tribe in the area. Through our interpreter, we planned with the Sakai Chief for his tribe to take us across the Pahang River in sampans. While we talked over the details, some bare-breasted young women served us tapioca cakes and coffee. As Bussy took one of the tapioca cakes from the young lady seated next to him, he looked over, smiled, and said, "It is not all bad in the jungle." Bussy gave Chief Pongulu some money and gold and the latest news to seal the deal. We felt good about our arrangements and left with the sense that the Chief's Sakai tribe at the river would take us across when the time came.

Bussy and I went back to camp and slept a few hours more. At dawn, we started walking again in rough jungle terrain in the pouring rain. We walked for eight hours until our Chinese escort guided us to a Chinese home, a predetermined stopover location. The Chinese homeowner told us to relax and wait, and there would be a high-ranking Communist Anti-Jap Army guerrilla coming soon to meet us.

Later that night, one of the Communist Anti-Jap officers from the Second Detachment, one of Lao Woo's right-hand men, came with a message for us. He said Lao Woo and the British Major would not be crossing the river and coming to this house, but they would meet us at the Second Detachment Camp on the other side of the Pahang River. The guides would escort us there.

With our guides and armed guerrillas, Bussy and I continued along an old elephant trail through the jungle until we reached a large Sakai camp on the edge of the Pahang River. At this village, there were 30 huts on stilts and one large main Sakai house, one of those long narrow bashas on stilts where several families lived. As before in the other Sakai camps, they watched our every move and fed us very well. Our guides let us know that the Sakai already heard from their Chief Pongulu, and they would take us across the Pahang River. But they wanted to wait until after dark because it would be too dangerous to cross in the daylight. Through the grapevine, the Sakai heard that the Japanese suspected we were in the area, and they had already sent hundreds of troops this way to look for us.

About midnight, the Sakai pulled two long sampans out of the undergrowth along the river's edge, and Bussy and I climbed in along with our two guides from the Second Detachment and the other two guerrillas. The Sakai pushed the sampans off the bank in almost pitch darkness. Roaring river currents caught the sampans and propelled us downstream in the swollen river. The Sakais' hand-carved paddles did not make a sound as they pushed the two sampans side by side out into the river.

It was a vast river, and we could not see the opposite shoreline in the black night. It took more than 20 fearful minutes for the powerful Sakai to paddle the sampans through the swift water to the opposite shore. When our guides jumped out, we followed them away from the river into the jungle. The sampans and the Sakai disappeared back into the night without a sound. The Sakai were terrific people. Since language kept us from communicating with them, we wondered why they helped us and not the Japanese in such a dangerous undertaking.

The guides found the trail that took us up a path and out of the jungle. Just minutes later, we came to the edge of a rubber plantation. The guides took us through long rows of rubber trees that shimmered with splendor in the pale moonlight. We walked along the many lines of trees for three hours until we came to an abandoned railroad. When we crossed the tracks, we stopped at a Chinese farmhouse on the other side. The guides talked with the farmer and his wife, and they allowed us to rest there for a while. We waited for dawn before heading back into the jungle. We kept a steady pace, crossing over many big steep hills. It was up and down terrain all that day, a very tough walk.

At 1:00 in the afternoon, we reached a road where the head guide stopped me, pointed ahead, and said, "Close! Close!" He motioned us with his hands to move fast. We crossed the road into a large open field in broad daylight and continued over open farmland for another hour. We soon arrived at a house on the other side of the farm. The Chinese farmer made us some tea and told us the house belonged to an Anti-Jap Army guerrilla. He said we could not go on to the Second Detachment Camp until we talked with Lao Woo. That resulted in a big argument between the Chinese farmer and me. I told our guides we wanted to keep moving on without delay to the Second Detachment camp.

You can imagine this Chinese-English argument. With nobody understanding anybody, we were not making much progress. At about 4:30 in the afternoon, a Chinese Communist Anti-Jap Army officer arrived to escort us to the Second Detachment Camp. We walked for two more hours and arrived at the jungle camp at about 6:30.

Two Australian Army Captains—Morrie and Robbie—came to meet Bussy and me when we arrived in camp and said their Commanding Officer, Major Leonard, would be along in a few days.

The first thing I did was ask Robbie, "Is your radio working? I want to send a message right away."

"Yes," Robbie replied. "Let's go there now."

I was now at a location where there was a radio!

The Detachment radio operator, a British enlisted man, sent my message to Allied Headquarters in Ceylon and the Twentieth Air Force (20th Bomber Command). He sent each message with Morse code in secret coded sequences.

The message included the names and serial numbers of my *Postville Express* crew members, the known status of each one, and my location. I also made sure they knew the urgency for a submarine pickup because of Duffy's health.

Bussy sent a separate message to his Force 136 Intelligence Group with his information. I am sure it surprised them to hear from him. We heard they declared him missing in action, and a few months after that, they reported him killed in action.

Robbie and Morrie were as glad to see us as we were to see them. They broke out a bottle of Scotch, and we celebrated with a few drinks. They told us they parachuted into the jungle a few weeks earlier and were part of the British Force 136 Intelligence Group. Their mission was to join the Anti-Jap Army guerrillas and help organize them to prepare for a British invasion of Malaya and Singapore.

Over drinks, Robbie and Morrie said they were having a great deal of trouble with Lao Woo. He wanted to run the complete show as the Malayan Communist Anti-Jap Army head and was not cooperating with them. Lao Woo also refused to salute the British flag. Robbie and Morrie made quite a big deal of this in their story to us. Lao Woo moved his Communist Party flag over to the other side of the camp's clearing. It appeared as though he wanted to set up his separate Communist Anti-Jap Army Headquarters.

Since they had just arrived, the British Force 136 Group received daily parachute drops with weapons and supplies for their new camp. Robbie and Morrie said the Anti-Jap guerrillas stole some guns that just arrived and stored them away for their Anti-Jap Army. We could not understand why the British wanted to arm or organize the guerrillas. After organizing and arming the Communist Army, there would only be more trouble for the British when this war was over.

Before the B-24 Liberators made any supply airdrops, the camp needed to communicate the details via radio to the pilots. The officer in charge gave the pilots the drop zone coordinates, what time they expected the scheduled drop, and the designated ground signal-fire patterns used for each scheduled drop.

The radio operator was having a hard time keeping the batteries charged that kept the radio operating. There were a lot of shipments of supplies scheduled for the coming days and weeks. And being in a Japanese-occupied country without communication was not a desirable situation. I knew that all too well.

The British parachuted in a gasoline generator and a steam generator as a backup. The radio operator now had to use the backup steam generator to charge the radio batteries. The much more efficient and easy to use gasoline generator had been running off and on. Then, it just quit altogether.

The radio operator always had to keep a small fire burning under the water tank to create the steam that turned the turbine to power the generator that charged the batteries. But now the steam generator was also on the blink.

When we first arrived, Bussy and I worked on the gasoline-powered generator, but after a quick try, it still would not run. We looked at the steam generator to see if it might run again. With some luck and with the radio operator's help, the steam generator was soon working. But to keep it operating full time, we had to take it apart and clean it once a day.

It would better to have the gasoline generator engine working because the steam generator was challenging to maintain and keep running. Having a working generator was vital because we always needed to be available with reliable full-time radio communication.

I inspected the gasoline engine for the generator and put my farm upbringing knowledge to work. Bussy and I took the gasoline engine apart and found that the intakes and exhaust ports were dirty. We cleaned them out and put it back together. It still would not run. Next, we put in new spark plugs, drained all the gasoline out of the tank and fuel line, and put in gas from another storage tank in the camp. The engine still would not run. We decided we must have contaminated gasoline because the engine should run. We told the radio operator to order a fresh supply of gas with the next airdrop.

While we worked on the gasoline engine, the British radio operator watched us in fascination and said he could not believe we took the engine apart, piece by piece. While he watched us, he told us that Commanding Officer Major Leonard did not like Americans. He thought we ought to know that before the Major arrived.

"Why doesn't Major Leonard like Americans?" I asked.

"Because you are colonists, and he doesn't like colonists," he answered.

In a few days, the new gasoline supply arrived by parachute. We filled the generator's fuel tank with the new fuel, and it ran like a top. Colonists or not, we were sure we would impress the Major who we were soon to meet.

The radio operator transmitted the radio messages in Morse code, and as part of a secret system, they sent only half a message at a time. A person on each end would decipher the transmissions. We had to wait until both halves arrived so the radio operator could solve the secret code and read the resulting message. The radio operator used one code for Major Leonard's communications and another code for all other communications.

On July 24th, Ceylon scheduled the camp to receive a parachute drop, and the drop zone (DZ) needed the ground signal-fires ready. Robbie needed some men, and he asked Bussy and me to go, so we went. We walked several miles through the jungle to where they had cut out an area for this DZ. We helped them build several big signal-fires in a prescribed pattern on the ground. Then at 6:30 that evening, a B-24 flew over the DZ right on time. The pilot did not see the signal-fires and went home without dropping the supplies. We went back to camp empty-handed that day.

A few days later, Major Leonard arrived in camp with Lt. "Tony" Tomlinson, Captain P. "Peter" Smith, and several Malay office-type helpers. Lao Woo went to find them and brought them back early because a sizable Japanese patrol was searching the Kuala Lipis area for us. Lao Woo thought they might find the Major's party while searching for us. So the Major's group came back much sooner than Robbie and Morrie expected.

Right away, Robbie and Morrie filled in Major Leonard on how Lao Woo moved his flag across the clearing to the other side of camp to establish a separate Communist Anti-Jap Army Headquarters. And he demanded to be the head of the Malayan Communist Anti-Jap Army and refused to salute the British flag. They also told him they thought the Chinese guerrillas were stealing from the British stockpile of guns.

Major Leonard went to Lao Woo and talked to him for quite a while. I do not know what the Major said, but he persuaded Lao Woo to cooperate. During their conversation, Major Leonard said Lao Woo assured him the Anti-Jap Army was not anti-British.

Lt. Tomlinson was an expert on the radio with Morse code and the secret code sequencing, and that night he deciphered all the messages from Ceylon Headquarters to us and from us to them. There were about 20 coded messages incoming, and several had gone out.

One radio message arrived telling Major Leonard they scheduled an airplane drop at 1800 hours with a medical doctor along with many medical supplies. The second part was an announcement. It said the U.S. Army had awarded Captain Franklin Bithos—or J. Jack Bussy, as we knew him—the Silver Star. They also congratulated him for still being alive.

I wished they would tell me the same, not the part about the Silver Star but an acknowledgment that they knew I was alive. That would have been sufficient. At least I would know Allied Headquarters knew I was still alive and was aware I had been living in the jungle since bailing out of the *Postville Express* and was now living with their British Force 136. I hoped they would advise our families upon receiving my original message, including our names and serial numbers. Eight months is a long time for a mother and father to have no news about their son except "missing in action."

That day I joined Robbie to help him at the DZ. We prepared the signal fires and then waited for the plane to arrive with the doctor. The pilot was on time, and the M.D. parachuted out, along with many other parachutes loaded with lots of medical supplies and a few Army supplies. We even received some recent *Time* magazines and several bottles of Scotch whiskey. While walking back to camp, the doctor and I had a pleasant conversation. He was Chinese, raised in Hong Kong, and received his medical training in England. He said he brought a lot of medicine and equipment to treat the Malay natives, Chinese natives, the Chinese Anti-Jap Army, and even the British, if needed.

It was late when we arrived back in camp, but everyone stayed up for several hours longer than usual talking to the doctor. Everyone wanted to know what he knew about the war. The men asked a lot of questions, and his answers were encouraging. It sounded like the war might be over soon, which meant all of us could go home.

When we awoke the next morning, there was a long waiting line on the main jungle trail that led to our camp. Most were Chinese women bringing their small children to have them treated by the doctor.

When the doctor saw the line, he asked if I would help while he treated all his newfound patients. I went with him while he set up his "office" in a small basha at the edge of the clearing. At least 30 to 40 patients were waiting in line. The doctor asked me to bring them inside one at a time.

The doctor examined each one and said malaria had infected most of them. He showed me where and how to check if a child had a swollen spleen caused by the disease. For the rest of the day, I helped check the children for malaria. The doctor gave the mothers a supply of Atabrine and told them in Chinese how to administer the pills to their children. They thanked the doctor and disappeared down the trail into the jungle. Patients arrived one after the other with many medical conditions. As the doctor looked at the long line, he said he hoped we had enough medicine for all the patients. Then he looked up with his tired eyes and added, "If I could only have one medication, it would be opium."

With the fast-tracking underground news about the doctor's arrival, the Chinese and Malay patients continued to arrive for the next several days. But the guerrilla guards reported no Japanese activity in the immediate area, even though word was that they were still searching for us.

This phenomenon had intrigued me during the last eight months. The Chinese, Sakai, and Malay grapevine could track us, hide us, and keep us informed about Japanese whereabouts without the Japanese ever being able to discover our exact location and capture us. It was almost miraculous.

On August 3rd, Major Leonard scheduled me to go to the DZ again. I woke up with a nasty ear infection. It was too painful for me to walk. Peter and Robbie took my place and said the planes flew over the DZ three times where three big signal-fires were going in the proper pattern, but the pilot never came down low enough to see them.

While Peter and Robbie were at the DZ, we received a radio message from the pilots. The pilots said they did not see or receive any signals from us, so they dumped seven large containers filled with food supplies into the sea. Major Leonard was not happy with this news because he needed food for the guerrillas, and he needed it soon. He promised to feed them as part of their deal, and he needed to keep that promise to keep Lao Woo and his Anti-Jap Army allegiant to the British.

On August 5th, Captain Peter Smith and I went to the DZ to receive another airdrop. We took some Communist guerrillas and some Sakai to package the cargo and carry it back to camp. A plane came right on time at 5:30 in the evening and dropped six large containers and four crates. The last parachute with a box of supplies landed in a tall tree. The Sakai climbed straight up the tree and brought the package down in five minutes. Watching a Sakai climb to the top of a 100-foot tree is an astonishing sight to see. The Sakai were a big help to Major Leonard and the Second Detachment.

When we returned to camp HQ, there were many radio messages for Major Leonard but only one brief bit of information for me. The short statement concerning me read, "Evacuation of Airmen unlikely." That was it.

I contacted Ceylon the first day I arrived regarding arranging a submarine ASAP because Duffy was so sick. Now, after receiving this return message, I sent another radio message explaining the seriousness of Duffy's condition and the need for his prompt rescue from the jungle.

I had walked 800 miles through the steaming jungle, 800 miles hoping to find a radio, and 800 miles praying we could contact someone to help Duffy. Imagine my disappointment. After 800 miles, I reached a radio and made contact, and Allied HQ only felt the need to respond, "Evacuation of Airmen unlikely." Disappointment does not even scrape the surface of all I thought at that moment.

Later that day, another new airdrop came in that kept me busy. Morrie, Robbie, and I went to the DZ with some guerrillas and Sakai to pick up the airdropped supplies. The aircraft missed the DZ again with three of the packages. Since they used camouflaged parachutes on this drop, they were almost impossible to find in the tall jungle trees.

We looked where we thought they landed, but we could not locate them. We asked several Sakai to help us, and they found all three parachutes in the treetops in just minutes. I watched one Sakai climb the trunk of a very tall tree about 125 feet high. He cut a package down and climbed on up to get the parachute tangled in the top limbs. It is astonishing to watch the Sakai at work.

The Sakai found the last box at the top of a tree they did not want to climb. To retrieve this box, they cut several smaller trees down that fell in a crisscross fashion to make a cradle of limbs. Then they cut the taller tree down, so it fell into the cradle of branches, and the package was undamaged. The Sakai accomplished this in less than an hour.

After we collected the three packages and chutes, Robbie, Morrie, and I sat down to rest on the limb of a large, downed tree. The Sakai ran over to us and motioned for us to move to a nearby log several feet away. After we walked over to their designated spot, they pointed to a large dead limb on the tree over the place where we had been sitting.

Our jungle survival book we kept in the parachute kit said the most dangerous thing in the jungle was falling trees and limbs. It said they were more hazardous to our lives than Bengal tigers, black panthers, elephants, and snakes. We were not paying enough attention to those instructions, but the Sakai, who lived in the jungle all their lives, were taking great care of us.

CHAPTER 15

Japan Surrenders

On August 10th, we received a radio message about a new atomic bomb the Americans had used against the Japanese. President Harry Truman ordered two bombs dropped on Japan, one on Hiroshima on August 6th and another on Nagasaki on August 9th. Reports stated the bombs almost wiped out both cities and would more than likely end the war. The next day, August 11th, we received some good news. The Japanese asked for a peace conference with only one condition—Hirohito would continue as Emperor of Japan.

Admiral Lord Louis Mountbatten, Supreme Allied Commander of

the South East Asia Command at Headquarters in Ceylon, sent us an updated message. It said the Allied Command sent their answer back to the Japanese and were now waiting for their response. But the war continued.

On August 12th, Bussy received a letter through a Chinese guerrilla runner from Wong Cheong Yiat asking him to return to the plantation. Wong Cheong Yiat's brother, Wong Cheong Kiat, was on his way from Kuala Lumpur and wanted to hide out at Bussy's camp in the jungle. The brother was terrified of what the Japs might do when the war ended. He wanted to stay out of sight and out of mind for a while. Bussy left that day to walk back to the tapioca plantation to receive Wong Cheong Yiat's older brother when he arrived.

We spent the next several days waiting and hoping to receive a radio message telling us the war was over. All we received was a message saying the United Nations was still awaiting a reply from the Japanese.

On August 14th, Robbie, Morrie, and I went to a new DZ site to build the signal-fires for a two-airplane supply drop. Major Leonard told the Sakai he wanted a new DZ site located farther from the camp and deeper into the jungle because of reports there were Japanese soldiers in the area. It took the Sakai one day to cut down the trees and clear the jungle brush to create the new DZ. The Sakai were hard workers, and they were efficient.

Both planes arrived together right on time, but they dropped their loads almost right in the middle of the signal-fire flames. The Sakai acted fast and grabbed the packages and removed them before the fire could damage them. The pilots circled, and each plane dropped four more large tin containers of rice. But these containers did not have parachutes, so they fell fast to the ground. One box landed within 15 feet of one of the Chinese guerrillas who did not see it coming. It could have been fatal.

This shipment included an enormous amount of food and supplies for the guerrilla soldiers and a large stockpile of K-rations. It surprised us to find a couple more bottles of Scotch cached in this delivery.

It rained hard most of the way as we walked back through the entangled jungle growth. Several Chinese bearers helped us carry the dropped packages, but because the DZ was farther away, it took us more than three hours of walking through thick brush to get back to camp. Arriving back at camp, I took off my damp shirt to dry off and found 10 to 12 leeches full of my blood on my back and stomach. As I looked down at the bulging parasites on my stomach, I thought to myself, "I hope I do not run out of blood before we run out of Japs."

On August 15th, we received the radio message we had all been waiting to hear. "The war is over!" Japan surrendered on August 14, 1945. The fighting stopped with plans for the Japanese to sign the terms of surrender with General Douglas MacArthur in Manila, Philippines.

There were still no messages from the US Army Air Force or the OSS, our intelligence agency, with instructions for my crew and me. The only news we received was a message to Major Leonard from the British Intelligence Agency, British Force 136, that said, "Do nothing until further orders arrive."

We dialed in the radio to see if we could hear any updates. The only news was that the Russians had entered the war, and the Japanese surrender party who were expected to sign the surrender papers in Manila had not yet left Japan.

Later that day, a runner arrived with a letter from Bussy. The letter said Bussy's man Angry had to shoot a Japanese soldier during a confrontation with a Jap patrol in front of the Plantation Office Building. He also said he seized the Sultan of Pahang's car and took the Sultan into the office building to question him. The letter said the Japanese had left their vicinity, and that the Sultan, Duffy, Saltzman, Wong Cheong Yiat, and a local doctor were hiding and safe in the Plantation Office Building. He heard about truckloads of Japanese soldiers armed with mortars and machine guns at the 89-mile post still attacking the tapioca plantation workers. He did not think these Jap soldiers knew the war was over.

Several days after the war ended, we still did not have any new

British HQ or US HQ orders.

We heard nothing more from Bussy, and I wondered if Duffy and Saltzman were okay. The radio news said the Japs announced a ceasefire order that went out to all Japanese forces on August 16th. They expected it would take at least a week for the ceasefire order to reach all areas of Malaya.

Major Leonard received a radio message from Mountbatten, the Supreme Allied Commanding Officer, instructing him to prepare to take over the areas evacuated by the Japanese Army as they retreated to the north. The British planned to move back into Malaya and therefore needed the allegiance of Lao Woo and his Communist Party Army.

With these new instructions in mind, Major Leonard put in an extra-large order for equipment and other supplies he would need for his job ahead. Since there were many large supply deliveries scheduled over the next days and weeks, the Major decided he needed a more extensive and closer location for the drops and storage. He thought a nearby rubber plantation would be a perfect location. He scheduled an airdrop of a massive amount of supplies, but there was no designated area at the enormous rubber estate cleared and ready for the drops. That same day, he sent Sakai into the rubber plantation to clear and prepare a site for the upcoming enormous drops of supplies.

Morrie and Robbie walked to the rubber plantation to supervise the Sakai and have a look around. They found two houses, a big one and a smaller one we could use for an office and sleeping quarters. With that news, everyone here planned to move into our new homes the next day. We also hoped to find a car or a truck so we could use its engine battery to charge the radio batteries and keep the radio going all the time.

Some local natives came from Jerantut, just up the road from the plantation. They told us about a group of terrified Jap soldiers in town who had barricaded themselves in the police station. They did not plan to come out until they knew the Americans and British would not shoot them. Somehow, these Japanese soldiers had already received news that they had lost the war and Japan had surrendered, but they did not know if we knew the war was over.

When we were preparing to move into the camp, I received these radio messages from Southeast Asia Command in Ceylon.

"Possible pickup by submarine off a surveyed coast."

"Port 'L' position five-mile suggested."

"Recognition only required."

"Discuss it with us as soon as possible."

"How long do you estimate your journey to coast?"

"The alternative is to land at the nearest airfield."

"Given the Japanese surrender, does Quack think Duffy could make it?"

"We can send plane pickup in three or four weeks."

"Port 'L' submarine unlikely to be earlier."

"If Quack requires specific drugs or equipment to treat Duffy, advise, and we'll send it."

I sent this radio message in reply: "Because of the Japanese surrender, we will wait and inform you of an airfield and a date for pickup. If possible, I prefer a plane from the 20th Bomber Command for pickup." I requested a plane from the 20th Bomber Command in hopes it would be quicker.

The next day, we all moved into the large plantation manager's home and the nearby smaller house on the rubber estate. This immense plantation was a Dunlop Rubber Plantation run by the British before the Japanese bombed Pearl Harbor and at almost the same time invaded Northern Malaya in December 1941.

The British cut these Malayan jungle plantations out of the middle of the dense jungle. After they cleared out all the trees and brush, they planted the rubber trees in straight rows. This plantation was old enough to have very impressive trees that were 50 to 60 feet tall. The bark on the rubber trees looked silvery and seemed to shimmer at night in the moonlight. They were beautiful.

A rubber worker, most likely a Chinese or Indian man because the Malay men would not work, went out each morning and carved a small

V deep into the bark of every rubber tree. Under the V, they drove in a U-shaped peg on which they hung a small cup. The latex ran down to the U-shaped peg from the new V cut in the bark and then dripped into the small cup. Each afternoon, the workers went down the rows of trees to empty the hundreds of sap-filled cups into a large bucket they carried. They took their full buckets of latex sap to a central area where they dried, treated, and rolled the latex into large bundles.

Before the war, they tapped these trees every morning. Now they had gone untapped for many months because the Japanese cargo ships could not ship the rubber out of the country. The Allies surrounded Malaya with a naval blockade that blocked all shipping in or out of all ports.

The Communist guerrillas set up a roadblock and hijacked a truck driving into the plantation so we could use its battery to keep the radio going full time. We organized the office in the house with the radio transmitter by a side window and parked the truck near the window. After we settled into our new quarters, we all sat down to a competitive poker game. I was a big winner of Straits dollars (Malayan currency) that night and maybe even won a few British pounds.

On August 26th, I received another radio message that all the 20th Bomber Command B-29s were busy, but the Royal Air Force was ready and willing to pick us up at any airport we named. When the Japanese left Jerantut and Kuantan, I planned to go to the Kuantan airstrip and arrange for a pickup. We did not know how fast that would happen, but we did receive a new radio message saying the Allied Command had ordered the Japanese to evacuate Singapore and Pahang and move north.

I was also waiting for more news from Bussy, Duffy, and Saltzman. I wanted an update on their status. We heard the Japs blew up the ferryboat crossing the Pahang River, and it had been out of commission the past four or five days. They could not use the ferry if they tried to come this way. We also received information confirming Bussy's letter about the lorry of Japanese soldiers at the 89-mile post, so that could also be the reason we had not yet heard from them. We hoped Bussy, Duffy, and Saltzman were hiding in safety from those Japs.

Radio contact was now continuous. We kept the batteries charged with the truck and contacted Ceylon at every scheduled time, day and night. The planned airdrops were coming daily. Two planes were due for a drop later today, but around noon, another message arrived. "No more plane drops the rest of today." That gave us a temporary break in the action. Next, a message came from the base at Columbo, Ceylon, and another from Mountbatten's Headquarters in Kandy, Ceylon, all wanting to know if we knew anything about the whereabouts of the Sultan of Pahang. There were reports he went missing between the 85- and 90-mile posts on the Kuantan Road.

On August 28th, two guerrillas arrived by bicycle with a letter from Bussy saying not to worry. They were all in the manager's house, and all were well. Everybody was thrilled to hear the news. It pleased everyone to receive the letter after hearing about the Japs at 89-mile post still fighting the war.

The next morning, I received a radio message that an airplane pickup for Saltzman, Duffy, and me depended on whether there was an airstrip big enough and long enough for a 20th Bomber Command B-29. Great! They found a B-29 to pick us up. The message instructed us to provide the location and the length of the runway at the airfield we chose. If no usable runways were available, they would try to pick up Duffy at the first opportunity by land, sea, or air after the Malaya overrun.

I hoped to find out from the Air Traffic Controller at the Kuala Lumpur Airport about usable landing airstrips in Malaya as soon as possible.

Another message came in for Major Leonard from Mountbatten. "Good job. Well done." This message was for Bussy concerning capturing and saving the Sultan.

Now I needed to get back to the plantation to pick up Duffy and Saltzman. I asked Major Leonard to write a letter to the Japanese Army commanding officer in Jerantut, asking for safe passage to the plantation. We needed the Japanese commander's assurance I could travel the Jerantut-Kuantan Road and use the ferry across the Pahang River without trouble from his troops. We also required a guarantee there would not be any trouble when I arrived at the 89-mile post to pick up Duffy, Saltzman, and Bussy.

Major Leonard sent a written letter to the Japanese commanding officer in Jerantut. He asked for peaceful passage on the Jerantut-Kuantan Road and the ferry across the Pahang River. The message also included a request for papers permitting us to pick up Saltzman, Duffy, and Bussy from the Japanese soldiers at the 89-mile post on the Kuantan Road. He told him they were waiting for us there at the tapioca plantation.

On August 30th, a runner delivered a return message to us from the Japanese commanding officer in Jerantut. The letter said only three men could come to his Jerantut Headquarters. We could only wear pistols, and we could not bring any other guns.

Later, we received another message through a native runner notifying us to come to tea at 11:00 a.m. Japanese time.

CHAPTER 16

Leaving Malaya

Several of us wanted to go to the Japanese tea event. I tried to convince Major Leonard that since the mission was to rescue my crew members, I should be the one to go. Major Leonard made us cut cards, and the three highest cards could go. Morrie, Robbie, and I were the winners.

We jumped into the truck parked beside the big house on the rubber estate and drove the few miles to Jerantut. It was a small town with only a few buildings. We went through the middle of the town square, found the police station, and parked the truck in front of the building. There was a soldiered and ready machine gun emplacement guarding the building on each side of the entrance walkway. When we—two tall Australian soldiers and one even taller American—stepped out of the truck, the Japanese soldiers swung their machine guns around and pointed them at us. I prayed they understood their orders and would follow them as we walked right past them and their machine guns up the walkway into the police station.

As we walked up the steps, the large front door opened, and there stood a Japanese non-com soldier holding the door open for us. He bowed and invited us in. We entered a small, almost empty front room. The only furniture in the room was a six-foot round wooden table surrounded by four hardwood chairs. The soldier motioned for us to sit down at the table, turned an about-face, and marched away. There was an uneasy silence for several minutes after the non-com soldier left us alone sitting in the empty room and disappeared out the rear door.

After waiting a few minutes, we were all startled when a side door banged open. A very fat, Kempeitai police officer came shuffling in, followed by his young male attendant. He introduced himself in perfect English and asked what he could do for us. This man was obese with greasy black hair and a thin mustache. He was a Kempeitai officer with a reputation for being brutal, and he looked like the evil demon-like figure we might have expected. It was also apparent that he was drunk.

I explained to him that some of my crew were at a tapioca plantation at the 89-mile post on the Kuantan Road surrounded by Japanese soldiers. I told him I wanted to pick them up and bring them back to our camp near here. He seemed to think that was a reasonable request and called for his attendant to bring us tea.

As we sat at the table drinking tea, he said there were many Japanese soldiers where the ferry crossed the Pahang River and also on the road to the 89-mile post. He would have to provide us with an escort for safe passage.

The officer maintained a stern and sinister demeanor during the conversation, but he complied with all our requests. The officer told us to return at 0800 hours, and he would have a lorry and some soldiers ready to take us to the 89-mile post. He would guarantee safe passage and send written orders to the 89-mile post officer in charge to release the Americans.

As we stood up to leave, he asked if there was anything else he could do for us. We asked for a table and chairs for the house where we were living. He said he would have them delivered that afternoon. Somehow, he knew where we were living.

He walked with us down the walkway and past the machine-gun nests to our truck. To our surprise, he bowed and scraped to us in front of all the soldiers. The people of the town who were there stared in amazement as we hopped back into the truck and drove off to our new HQ at the rubber plantation.

The situation was very touchy because the war had been over for several days. However, Count Hisaichi Terauchi, the Japanese officer who oversaw all Southeast Asia, refused to accept the Emperor's instructions to surrender. The Count, a kind of royalty, stated Japan never lost a battle in the home islands and would not lose now after all these centuries. We did not know what the Japanese officers at the 89-mile post would do when we arrived to pick up Duffy, Saltzman, and Bussy.

I waited until the next day, September 1st, for the Jap escort to be available to go pick up Duffy, Saltzman, and Bussy. When Robbie, Morrie, and I arrived at 8:00 in the morning, we found two large lorries parked in front of the machine-gun nests in the town square. Around 10 Japanese soldiers were standing in the back of each truck with rifles in hand. The Kempeitai commanding officer came out of the building to meet us. He handed me a letter he wrote to the Japanese officer in charge at the 89-mile post. It told him to allow us to pick up Duffy, Saltzman, and Bussy. He also gave me another written message to give to the Jap non-commissioned officer in charge at the ferry crossing to allow our passage across the river. Robbie hopped in the cab of one truck with the driver, and Morrie and I jumped in the open back of the same lorry with about eight Jap soldiers.

The two trucks left the town of Jerantut, and we were on our way to the ferry where we would cross the Pahang River. After driving a short time on the main road, we approached the river. There was a long downhill incline to the river where the trucks needed to slow down to about 10 miles per hour. The road cut through the riverbank, leaving 10-foot-high embankments on each side of the entrance. A sizable rustic building lined the hill on the right, and Japanese soldiers lined the hilltop above us on the left.

When the soldiers saw us standing in the back of the truck as we rode by, they all started yelling and aiming their rifles straight at us. The driver slammed on the brakes, and the Jap officer in charge jumped out and began screaming commands at the soldiers on the embankment. Morrie and I expected the bullets to fly at any moment, but whatever the Japanese officer said quieted the soldiers down.

We pulled up to a massive ferry crossing building and parked. The Japanese officer in charge of our lorry stepped out of the driver's seat and motioned for Robbie, Morrie, and me to follow him into the building. All the Jap soldiers stayed behind in the truck.

As we entered the building, he stopped and pointed across to the ferry docked on the other side of the vast Pahang River. It seemed we had to wait for the ferryboat to come to this side of the river before we could cross. He could not speak any English, and none of us could speak Japanese, so it was an awkward situation. We were more than a little apprehensive. Jap soldiers were everywhere. He took us to a large room filled with wooden tables and benches, all jammed with Japanese soldiers. We wound through all the soldier-filled chairs and benches to an empty table, and he motioned for the three of us to sit down. When he walked away, I felt like every eye in the entire building was on us. Nobody said a word. There was total silence. After several tense minutes, our Japanese officer returned with four cups of hot coffee and joined us at the table. He smiled and said something to the Japanese soldiers. They all smiled back and started talking to one another again.

The three of us simultaneously said thank you in English to our coffee-bearing Japanese friend and gave him what we hoped was a reassuring smile. He only gave us a curt nod of his head and then turned his chair and started talking to some soldiers at the next table.

Robbie, Morrie, and I started talking about the situation at hand. We appeared as relaxed as possible as if we thought nothing of having coffee with 200 armed enemy soldiers. We laughed and joked about it among ourselves.

At the far end of the coffeehouse, about 50 feet away, a tall Japanese officer stood up and walked across the room toward us. When he reached our table, he stopped in front of us, clicked his heels, and bowed. He seemed to be a high-ranking officer, dressed in what looked like a brand-new tan gabardine uniform with shined leather boots. He was wearing a Sam Browne type leather belt, and a long silver Samurai sword hung at his side, almost touching the floor. The officer was tall for a Japanese with an imposing presence. When he stopped at our table, the two Australian officers and I stood up at attention, and I said, "Good morning."

He responded with "Good morning" in perfect English and said, "This is a sad day for the Japanese."

"Please join us for a cup of coffee," I said. "We know this may be a sad day for the Japanese, but it's a good day for everyone because the war is over."

He stood for a few moments and said again, "This is a sad day for the Japanese." He clicked his heels, gave a slight bow, and walked away to his table across the room.

After almost four years of war that almost cost us our lives and cost the lives of 50–60 million other human beings, the officer's response to us—three of his former enemies—was shocking. It did not feel like a response to losing a world war. It was almost like, "The ballgame is over, and we acknowledge the victor." But after living with Asians for nearly a year under very intimate conditions, I came to realize their value of human life.

After an hour, our Japanese officer stood up and motioned us to go with him out to the trucks. We climbed back into the lorry with the Japanese soldiers and rode down to the river's edge where there was a long pontoon barge tied to the dock. They drove the trucks onto the long, wide ferry boat barge. The ferry moved away from shore as Chinese coolies pulled the barge to the opposite side of the river. Thirty minutes later, we drove off our ferry boat and started down the road toward the plantation. With no trouble from the Japanese along the way, we reached the 89-mile post where we turned off the main road into Wong Cheong Yiat's tapioca plantation.

As soon as we entered the plantation, several Japanese soldiers with rifles stopped the trucks and started talking to the drivers. They spoke in Japanese for several minutes, and then one soldier left and came right back with an officer who appeared to be in charge. That officer read the orders and motioned each driver forward to the side of a nearby plantation building where the trucks stopped. As soon as we hopped off the lorry, we saw Duffy, Saltzman, and Bussy coming at us from around the corner, running as fast as their skinny and undernourished bodies could take them.

They were excited to see us, and I was excited to see them safe and sound. When I asked, "Are you ready to head back to the British camp where there is a radio?" Bussy yelled, "Let's get out of here! Pronto!"

Saltz said, "Hump, follow me over here. I want to show you something." He took me to the edge of the jungle where they hid the Sultan of Pahang's 1940 Packard convertible.

I said, "Very nice! Take it along with us!"

With that said, Saltzman jumped in the driver's seat and said, "Let's go, boys!" Duffy jumped in the passenger seat, and Bussy jumped in the back seat and yelled, "Let's go!"

"Bussy!" I shouted. "Where are Angry, Khaki, and Yapper? Are they coming?"

Bussy yelled out of the back seat as we were pulling out. "Come on, boys! Where are you? Hop in the lorry!"

Bussy's three Chinese boys came running and hopped in the back of the other lorry with the Japanese soldiers.

I said, "I want to stop by Wong Cheong Yiat's house to say goodbye. Follow us to the house."

We drove up the road to his house, and I knocked on the door. When Wong Cheong Yiat answered the door, I said, "We are all going back to the Second Detachment now. I wanted to say goodbye and thank you for everything you have done for us."

"It was my honor," Wong Cheong Yiat answered.

Then Bussy jumped in, "Yiat, Buddy, I'll miss you!" Then he jumped out of the back seat and gave Wong Cheong Yiat a big hug, lifting his feet off the ground.

"Captain Bussy," Wong Cheong Yiat said with a big smile, "It was both interesting and a pleasure to be in your company. I will never forget you, my friend."

Then Duffy and Saltzman said their goodbyes and thanked Wong Cheong Yiat for everything he had done for them. There were even a few tears shed as we left the tapioca plantation and headed north.

Saltzman drove the Packard with Duffy and Bussy. They followed behind the first truck with Bussy's boys and some Jap soldiers in the back. Robbie, Morrie, and I jumped in the back of the second truck with seven Jap soldiers and followed behind the Packard.

The beautiful 1940 baby blue Packard 120 Convertible Coupe looked out of place sandwiched between the two drab Japanese lorries as we drove up the main Jerantut-Kuantan Road back to the ferry.

The Japanese soldiers in the back of the truck started talking among themselves, putting their hands level with the tops of their heads and pointing at our heads, showing how much taller Robbie and I were. I took a pack of cigarettes out of my pocket and lit one up. I then offered each of the soldiers a cigarette and a light. They seemed to think my gesture of friendship was a great idea and accepted the offer. We drove back to Jerantut with the seven Jap soldiers, all smiling and smoking as if we were on a Sunday evening drive.

We made it back to Jerantut and pulled into the town square, and all the Japanese soldiers jumped out. I hopped off my lorry and squeezed into the Packard with Duff, Saltz, and Bussy. Bussy's three boys got into the back of the truck with Robbie and Morrie, and we all drove back to the new British HQ at the rubber plantation. It was a long day of driving, so we all found a bed somewhere in the house and drifted off to sleep.

Early the next morning, we went to Major Leonard's office, and I introduced Duffy and Saltzman to the Major and the others. Bussy was already in the office standing off to the side with a big smile on his face like he knew something I did not. I asked Major Leonard if there was any recent information for me.

He said, "Good news, gentlemen. I have a driver waiting outside to take the three of you to Singapore. As soon as you arrive in Singapore, make a call, and ask the operator for the American Army officer in charge. They will take care of you there. Maybe I will catch up after I'm finished here with the Japs."

"That is excellent news, Major! I will be happy to leave you to your work," I joked. "Thank you for everything, Major."

"Are you coming with us, Bussy?" I asked.

"No, it looks like I will head back on October 15th. We'll touch base and have a brandy when I get back to the States." Bussy had the usual smile on his face as we walked out the door.

Saltzman, Duffy, and I went outside to meet our new Malay driver. We stuffed ourselves into the Packard and started on our way to Singapore and our flight home.

The trip to Singapore was 350 miles, including a slight detour. About halfway there, we wanted to stop by Kota, the village where Talib lived. Talib was the Malay Headman who first guided us away from the crash site and saved our lives by helping us escape from the Japs. The driver said it was not far out of the way and agreed to take us there.

As we approached the small village of Kota, the driver stopped to ask a native Malay if he could find Talib so we could talk with him and thank him. The local man told our driver that when the Japanese came to this area looking for us and could not find and capture us, they killed every man and boy in the village. What a waste of a courageous man and his sons. They died to save us. We rode on thinking about what might have happened during these past months without the incredible people we met along the way. Although they owed us nothing, they helped in whatever ways they could. Their pure generosity is why I can write this story.

In contrast to the cheerful way we had celebrated that morning when we enjoyed starting our trip back to freedom, we were now in a melancholy mood. Freedom! What a beautiful word! Few people have lived imprisoned in a jungle for this long, and this experience gave me an even better appreciation for the word *freedom*.

We rode past rubber plantations, through the tall trees of the Malayan jungle, through the hills where the natives grew tea for export, and past the Chinese and British tea houses. I was reminiscing about our time in the jungle when we rounded a steep curve in the road and heard guns going off ahead of us. The driver slammed on the brakes and said he was too scared to go any farther.

We discussed the situation with the driver and learned that the Malays, the Chinese, and some Indians were in a battle to control the area. They knew the defeated Japanese were moving out, and each of them wanted to be the ruling government after the Japanese evacuated.

After a few minutes, the shooting stopped, and we persuaded the driver to move ahead. I pulled out a big wad of Straits dollars and waved them in front of the Malay driver's face—the magic potion for getting things done in Malaya. I assured him he would receive a substantial reward when he deposited us in Singapore.

He drove ahead cautiously. Soon we were going by the area where the shooting took place, and our driver, now terrified, pressed down on the accelerator to speed up the car as fast as possible to put the fighting behind us. He said we were lucky to get away because now there was a civil war with no police or government, just chaos.

We rode on for miles through low swampland and jungle on both sides of us. We did not see any natives anywhere, and there was no traffic on the roadway.

It was dark as we approached the Straits of Johor, the water that separates Malaya from the island that is the city of Singapore. As we neared the road leading us to the causeway to cross the Straits of Johor to Singapore, we saw hundreds of Japanese soldiers bivouacked along both sides of the road. There were rifles stacked here and there along the way. Tents lined the road for miles. We were three skinny white Americans emaciated from our hiding in the jungle for eight months and now surrounded by thousands of Japanese soldiers staring at us as we passed by. The soldiers studied us as they smoked their cigarettes in small groups along the sides of the road.

We were quiet as we contemplated what could happen if one or more of them decided they did not like being the defeated enemy. The Japanese still needed to sign the surrender documents, but the British had already ordered the Japanese Army troops out of Singapore. Multitudes of soldiers camped along the road in tents, waiting for further orders. There were hundreds of trucks, staff cars, artillery pieces, farm carts, and every other type of vehicle jammed along the highway for 15 miles or more. Everywhere we looked, there were cooking fires surrounded by Japanese soldiers.

We moved through this bottleneck of men and vehicles at about five miles per hour. And here was the astonishing thing. Although we were only three armed men amid thousands of defeated Japanese soldiers, they did not harass us.

As we drove up to the entrance to cross the Strait, there were no more Japanese. The driver proceeded across the causeway, the same path the Japanese used to invade Singapore's British fortress just four years earlier. As we left the south end of the causeway on the other side of the Straits of Johor, we entered the city. It was now late at night. There was no activity, no cars, no people, and very few lights.

Our Malay driver did not know where he was going. He drove along until we came to a gasoline station, and I asked the driver to stop. I entered the station and asked if there was a phone I could use. The Malay native studied me head to toe. I will admit I did not look like much with my hand-me-down native shirt and torn pants. I was also as skinny as a rail, but I had my Maple Leaf of Army Rank pinned to my collar.

He pointed to the phone on the outside wall and gave me some coins to use. I dialed the operator who answered in Malay. I asked to talk to the American Army officer in charge. She chattered with someone for a few moments in Malay, and then there was silence. Minutes later, a man answered in English. I told him who we were and that my instructions were to call the American Army officer in charge when we arrived. After another few minutes, another Limey came on the phone and said, "I will try to find an American. Hang on, please."

After several more minutes, an American, Officer Major Smith, came on the phone. After I told him who we were and where we were, he said, "Come on into Singapore. Go to the Adelphi Hotel. Eat anything you want there at the hotel, and the Army will get the bill. A staff car will pick you up in front of the hotel in the morning at 9:00."

Off we went to downtown Singapore with our driver stopping to ask directions every few minutes. It was just after midnight when our driver stopped at a small building that looked ancient and unkempt on the outside. We trusted our Malay driver when he said it was the Adelphi Hotel and got out in front of the old building. I gave our Malay driver a big wad of Straits dollars and told him thanks. I asked him to please deliver the Packard back to Wong Cheong Yiat, and he will know where to return the vehicle to the Sultan of Pahang.

We walked up a narrow wooden stairway to enter the hotel's small lobby with a small reception desk. A dark-skinned Malay young man was sitting behind the counter. He looked us over and asked what he could do for us. I told him our orders were to sleep at this hotel for the night, and we needed three rooms. I explained we were American Army Air Corps officers and looked like this because we had been living in the jungle for eight months. He looked at us with a sleepy stare and said there were no rooms available.

I did not blame him because we looked like anything but Army officers. We were all wearing torn native shirts and trousers, worn-out shoes, and a bag of meager possessions tied to a stick slung over our shoulders. Even an American soldier would doubt the authenticity of my claim.

Since we were all tired and needed a bed, I told him again in a friendly way that our orders came from Major Smith. He ordered us to sleep at this hotel for the night, and he would pick us up here at 9:00 a.m. Then we would be out of his hair. He repeated, stronger this time, that there were no vacant rooms, and we could not stay there for the night.

I looked at the counter. It was a typical old hotel front desk with a hinged top that lifted to allow the clerk to enter behind the counter. I reached over, raised the countertop, and walked behind the counter. In front of me, hanging on the wall, was a row of keys with room numbers. I looked at the wide-eyed young man, handed Saltz a key, Duffy another, took one for myself, and said, "Please call us for breakfast."

It was a small place, so it was easy to find our room numbers on the hotel doors. We were all asleep in minutes.

Someone knocked on the door in the morning and announced, "Breakfast served in 10 minutes."

We washed in a bowl on the desk in our rooms to make ourselves as presentable as possible. We went past the front desk into the dining room, a very spacious and pleasant setting. A Malay boy came forward to seat us at a table. He presented us with a menu with entrees we had not seen or eaten in months.

A server brought us coffee and took our orders. We ordered fresh fruit and some of everything else, enjoying our first foray into real civilization in a long time. It was a large dining room with several tables, each with beautiful china and linen.

We were enjoying ourselves, sitting at our table drinking coffee and talking about the change from jungle fare, when a British Naval officer stood up from another table at the far end of the room. He walked over to us and stopped. The tall, slender British officer was resplendent in a starched white uniform and British Naval insignia. We stood up. He popped to attention, demanding to know who we were and what we were doing in the Royal Navy mess.

Understanding we were disreputable-looking characters compared to a British Naval officer, I explained, "We are American Army Air

Force officers, and the American Civil Affairs Officer ordered us to stay here for the night."

He responded, "What the hell has civil affairs to do with the Royal Navy? The Admiral requests that you leave."

He did a proper about-face and strode back to the Admiral's table to report his findings.

In a few minutes, the server brought us our magnificent breakfast, and we were enjoying our first civilized meal out of the jungle when the young Naval officer appeared again in a great huff.

"Whoever you are, the Admiral requests you leave the Royal Navy mess."

I stood up and introduced myself again and said, "Officer Major Smith ordered us here, and a staff car will pick us up here at 9:00. Tell the Admiral we will obey our orders and remain here until picked up at 9:00."

The British Naval officer spun around and returned to the Admiral's table. We did not hear another thing from them. We finished our splendid breakfast and at 9:00 went down to the staff car that was waiting for us. The Sergeant jumped from behind the wheel of the Army staff car and opened the doors for us. I thanked the Sergeant, and we jumped into the car. He said his orders were to take the three of us to the Governor's mansion.

We rode off in chauffeured style in contrast to walking barefoot in the jungle slime. It was a welcome change of transportation. After a few minutes, the driver turned into a driveway that went into a long, curved roadway around a high hill up to where the Governor's mansion stood. It looked just like it should, a massive structure with many tall white pillars in a curve around the front of the building.

The driver wheeled into the open area in front of the main foyer. The Sergeant opened our doors, and as we stepped out of the staff car, the mansion's main entrance door opened. There stood General Wheeler, the Deputy Allied Commander South East Asia, to welcome us.

General Wheeler invited us to sit down at a large, polished wooden table in the foyer. He said all he knew was that we were in the jungle for some time and it delighted him to welcome us back into the care of the U.S. Army.

He wanted to know how we fared last night at the hotel. When we told him about our reception by the British Navy at breakfast, he stood up, excused himself, walked up a long spiral staircase, and disappeared into the inner sanctum of the second floor. We sat in the foyer, marveling at how we were now enjoying such a change from the dark jungle. After a few minutes, General Wheeler came back down the spiral staircase and said, "I don't think you will have to worry about that Admiral anymore."

He wanted to know about our bombing experience and our stay in the jungle. He seemed interested in our well-being and said he would make reservations for us to stay at the Raffles Hotel until they could arrange our flight to the U.S. Army Hospital in Calcutta. He said the U.S. Air Transport Command would send a C-54 four-engine transport plane to take us to Calcutta where we could join four of our crew members who had just been released from a Japanese prison camp. He said radar man 1st Lt. Martin Govednik, left gunner Tech Sgt. Harold A. Gillett, top gunner Staff Sgt. John A. MacDonald, and right gunner Tech Sgt. Ralph Lindley were waiting for us at the Calcutta hospital.

It was wonderful to hear that some of my crew were alive and safe in the Calcutta hospital and that I would join them soon. I thanked the General for giving me the good news. I would later mourn the loss of my crew members who didn't come home—my co-pilot Lt. Col. Robinson Billings and radioman Tech Sgt. Michael Kundrat who died in the crash; rear gunner Staff Sgt. Rouhier E. Spratt who was severely burned and then died in the jungle within a few days; and Capt. Carl Hansman, our navigator, who died of malaria, cholera, and typhoid in a guerrilla camp in the jungle one month after our plane went down.

Our driver transported us to the Raffles Hotel, the most famous of all the hotels in Singapore. During our stay, we visited all of Singapore. The British were preparing the government buildings, the grounds, and the downtown area to be ready for the formal surrender ceremonies on September 12, 1945. They took all the British and Chinese prisoners just freed from the infamous Changi Prison and gave them authority over their former Japanese guards. The old British and Chinese prisoners now gave the one-time Japanese prison guards orders to clean the entire government area and downtown city area to prepare for the surrender ceremony. They clipped every blade of grass to perfection. Every building was shining, and every open space was spic and span.

We could not stay for the surrender ceremony because our plane came to take us to the hospital in Calcutta. They transported us to the Singapore Airport, and there sat a shining C-54 four-engine transport plane ready to pick us up.

As I walked up the ladder to take my seat in the plane, a Sergeant came running from the far interior of the aircraft and said, "Colonel Humphrey?"

Surprised by my new rank, and I replied, "Yes."

He handed me a bottle of Kentucky's finest bourbon and said, "Colonel Red Forman says, 'Welcome home.'"

What beautiful words—Welcome home!

* * *

I hope you enjoyed *8 Miraculous Months in the Malayan Jungle*.

Now that you have finished reading the book, it would be a big favor to me, and future readers, if you left feedback on Amazon. While I have no expectations on what kind of review you will leave, it would make my day knowing you read the book and shared your honest experience with the world.

You can post a review on www.Amazon.com

Thank you,

Donald J. "DJ" Humphrey II

Made in the USA
Monee, IL
22 February 2021